Distilled Spirits and Art: Handbook [2 Boo

An Illustrated Guidebook to Make Your Own Liquor, Wines or Beers Safely and Legally (Tips and Tricks on a Budget)

Don Pablo

Table of Contents

HOW TO MAKE HOMEMADE MOONSHINE, WHISKY, RUM AND OTHER DISTILLED SPIRITS

THE LOST HANDBOOK OF ARTISANAL BREWING

How to Make Homemade Moonshine, Whisky, Rum and other Distilled spirits

The Complete Guidebook to Make Your Liquor, Safely and Legally (Tips and Tricks on a budget)

Don Pablo

Disclaimer and Terms of Use: Effort has been made to ensure that the information in this book is accurate and complete, however, the author and the publisher do not warrant the accuracy of the information, text and graphics contained within the book due to the rapidly changing nature of science, research, known and unknown facts and internet.

Table of Contents

Introduction

Distillation at home is possible, and it is one of the best ways of getting your unique blend and brand of your preferred alcoholic beverage. This material will introduce you to the concept of distillation at home.

You can make all of these: moonshine, whisky, rum, vodka, wine, Pasco, soju, bacon, eau de vie, mescal, brandy, and more.

The process of making alcohol at home is not complicated, as long as you have some technical know-how and some basic equipment. With the right tools and a little know-how, you can make top-quality distilled spirits right in your very own kitchen.

Distilled alcohol is not only an excellent way to impress friends and family at your next dinner party, but it is also an age-old process that can have many therapeutic benefits.

Also, there are a large number of health benefits to consuming distilled alcohol, and most recipes also require you to boil the mixture for a while to dissolve the medicinal properties from the herbs and fruits. By the time you get to the end of a DIY distillation of any sort, you can be sure that only the most desirable essence of given alcohol is left behind, while not only removing most of the toxins and impurities, but also the headache-inducing congeners that wreak havoc on your head.

One of the main benefits of distillation over other medicinal preparations for healing is that it allows you to remove anything from your alcohol that you don't want to drink. Many people leave salts, caramel coloring, and other tinted substances in their liquor thinking that they might taste better, that is short-sighted.

Distilled alcohol is also not as taxing on the body as folk medicine, as it doesn't contain any medicinal ingredients. However, many people also claim that their health improves when they drink their homemade stuff, and there are numerous documented medical benefits.

This guide includes step-by-step written instructions for making moonshine and a variety of other high-quality alcoholic beverages.

A SHORT HISTORY OF SPIRITS AND THE DEVELOPMENT OF DISTILLATION

-Spirits have been consumed since the beginning of time, in a variety of ways. The earliest methods to devise alcohol were simply to ferment a raw foodstuff thoroughly, then strain it out and drink the remaining liquid. The first true distillation took place in India in 430 BCE. Alcohol was obtained by mixing grapes with hot sand, then distilling the fermented juice.

They slowly worked out the science and art of distillation. This process was used in Ancient Greece, which was first used to purify wine and create sweet wine.

But the process got a big boost in Britain later. The British had conquered parts of France and needed the fuel. They looked for other options and had the wits to extract a byproduct from the making of bread and beer. They then used the distilled fuel as fuel in their ships. British Steamship Shipping was immediately made an industry.

Today, the Netherlands and Italy are the largest producers of distilled alcohol on the planet.

Chapter 1: Homemade distillation

The simplest way to make alcohol at home is to start with homemade stills. Distillation is the process that allows you to separate liquids based on their physical properties.

The molecules in all alcoholic beverages have a certain boiling point and form a distinct layer on the surface when they begin to boil. This means that you can separate these water-based mixtures by creating a situation where a liquid boils before water vapor boils.

In theory, you can boil the components of several different beverages until you obtain the one type of alcohol in particular, with a purity of 95% at most. There is also a legend of a distillation process that produced 190-proof liquor.

Of course, this can only be accomplished by buying a still and obtaining high-quality alcohol, to begin with. But, as you will learn in the following guides, you can use other means to create distilled alcohol, and the techniques employed will be the same in all the processes that you will read about.

Good quality alcohol begins with the right yeast and the right carbs. Commercially prepared American vodka is about as pure as it gets, and the craft distillers of Europe also produce their products with high purity and quality.

But if you make your still, you will be able to achieve the same high quality on your own. However, some procedures may help you get the best results that require more time, more effort, and more money.

Volatile aroma compounds are also released, that is why we should not forget to mention the fact that the flavor of the end product will also be different.

If you use fresh potatoes, carrots, and raisins for fermentation, you will get liquor with a wonderful taste that you can enjoy just on its own, as well as a host of other health benefits.

Spirits are mostly used in cocktails or mixed drinks, or as a drink on their own. The term 'spirit' is generally used to refer to pure alcohol by itself, not to any mixing cocktail. spirits can be distilled from any liquid.

The process of distillation is simple, and it can produce a completely drinkable alcoholic beverage without any further help in the form of aging.

The oldest and most popular white liquor to be distilled is moonshine, that is distilled beer. In the United States, it is called mountain dew, and the first one was brewed in 1839–1840.

Whiskey is perhaps the liquor made most often by amateurs. There is nothing unusual about making your whiskey. All you need is the right equipment and the right ingredients.

The whiskey that you make won't be as strong as the ones that are purchased, and you will be technically considered a moonshine distiller. This is more of a geographical than a technical term, and it is perfectly all right to 'make booze' at home.

And the best part, you can make it yourself. Homemade liquors are cheaper, and they are healthier, too. There is nothing like tasting the sweetness of the sunrays of a summer vacation or the taste of homemade snow in the winter.

Chapter 2: Distillation equipment to make a distilled spirit

There are two ways for distilling alcoholic beverages, either as mash or directly from the fermented wash. The older ways of distilling used fermented wash, but nowadays it is more common to use mash. Distilling from the mash is more complicated to do and requires more equipment and materials. The sold fermented wash is more readily available and easy to use. When distilling fermented wash, the basic idea is to let the wash ferment until it has produced a certain percentage of alcohol, and then distill it. When distilling from the mash, you should start by aging it, and then distill it.

Age it

To increase the percentage of alcohol in the fermented wash you must "age" the wash, during which time the alcohol all gets converted to add sugar. Aged wash is neither alcoholic nor imbibed in the same way as other cleans. Aged wash can be aged further by adding more ingredients.

You could add concentrated beer or alcohol to the wash, which helps with the aging process. Generally, hard alcohol gives a better result in two stages than mild alcohol. Try to avoid high-alcohol beverages, such as vodka or whiskey, because these add alcohol to the wash, which can increase the percentage of alcohol in the distilled wash, but also produce an even more poisonous spirit. Harder and milder alcohols aged in wash produce better quality distilled wash than a stronger but equally "hard" alcohol.

Wash made from beets (spirits distilled from beet) is an exception as beet alcohol is highly poisonous when distilled.

Be sure to heat the wash to 80 Fahrenheit between distillations. Trim the wash must be heated until all the water in it has been evaporated.

As the wash ages, it needs to be heated regularly to keep it heated. If you fail to do this, the wash may be done aging, that is a good thing, but your distiller will get damaged. There are various ways to fix this, the most common way is to add water or alcohol to the wash, and it will be able to continue.

Types of Alcohol You Can Distill From

Fermented Wash

The Fermented wash is a liquid that is easy to make. This is the type of wash the majority of amateur distilleries are set up to use.

Fermented wash must have a minimum alcohol content of 5% to work. Fermented wash aged for a long time will have higher alcohol content.

Mash

Mash is a beverage made from the spent grain of the distillation process. Mash is what the words "mead", "sparkling wine", and "beer" actually refer to. Mash is more advanced than fermented wash because it has more ingredients. The mash used in a home distillery does not need to ferment much, in fact, having a living yeast can lead to off-flavors. One of the biggest differences between mash and fermented wash is the type of yeast used.

Mash has almost the same ingredients as a fermented wash, except it usually has yeast and more sugar. If the mash has too much sugar, it may produce an over-alcoholized wash. Mash is usually aged.

Distillation and Distillate

The distillation process separates the wash into its different components. Distillation starts when the fermented wash or mash is boiled. As the alcohol starts boiling, it rises to the top of the vat. The vapors are lowered again into the fermented. The low temperature of the mash allows the alcohol to vaporize. When the alcohol vapor reaches the bottom of the vat it condenses. This condensation is called the distillate.

The distillate should be stored cold, so it can tolerate high humidity and increase its aging time. In the beginning, one and a half times the amount of distillate should be added to the wash. This is called as head distillate. After a few hours, you should add a quarter of the amount of distillate. This is called tails distillate. After yet another few hours your distillate will be ready that you can boil and reduce it to a final product.

A distilled spirit keeps well for a long time, which gives you time to build a good supply. Over time, the aging of the spirit will potentially increase the alcohol level in the spirit.

Distilling Equipment and Materials

The Fermented wash contains all the ingredients you should need to distill, but if you are distilling a mash you will need additional equipment and materials.

The equipment you need to distill fermented wash is copper still. The Copper still should be made as a pot still. This is a still in which the fermented alcohol or mash is heated by direct fire or steam. The still is placed on a fire source, such as an oven or hot plate, because it has a fire or steam tube attached. The still must be made by very experienced blacksmiths. The still and its parts are made of steel. The excess fire tube should be made of copper.

A stove for distilling mash is very simple. It is a small furnace into which the needed fire tube is placed. The distillate is boiled off in the fire tube. The distillate then goes through the still and into another furnace. This is used to condense the steam.

The equipment required for either distilling method will be summarized as follows:

Equipment:

1. Operating table for distilling

2. Distillation sheet

3. Mash bucket

4. Star car

5. Measuring glasses

6. Measuring cup

7. Bins

8. Fermentation buckets

9. Copper pot

10. Copper pot lid

11. Toolbox

12. Fire

13. Mash

14. Distillate

15. Refill

16. Heat

17. Steamer

18. Mirrors

19. Watches

20. Brazier

21. Wash bucket

22. Refill

23. Additional glass

24. Fusel oil cake

25. Fibreglass

26. Mash tuba

27. Mash ampoules

The following equipment is needed to make mash:

Good, strong, highly heat-resistant copper.

A copper pot (or another container)

Galvanized steel gauze (or copper)

Glasses

Water

Copper faucet

Before distilling, you should be sure to take note of the following:

They are both similar in price, but the fermented wash is more commonly used in home distillations. The difference in cost between the two consumable items is based on a basic calculation.

Fermented wash seldom comes with the addition of yeast, but yeast used in your mash will be aged after boiling. Thus, you will have to buy your yeast after boiling as well. The yeast is a mix of batter, yeast granules, and carbon dioxide. Adding yeast to a ferment will activate this yeast and re-synthesize the alcohol. The yeast is added to the mash (fermented wash) and mixed thoroughly.

The Fermented wash is not normally fermented much after distillation. Properly prepared fermented wash has only a small amount of yeast and is therefore not affected after distillation. You should, however, be careful to keep your stock.

Chapter 3: How to make Moonshine

Moonshine is a popular alcoholic beverage consumed by millions of people, a significant reason why it is so popular is because of the unique blends that go into the production process. Remember to enjoy all alcoholic beverages responsibly to avoid alcoholic abuse.

Most of the time to create your alcoholic beverage at home, you will need to start with the base, that is always the mash. Some people who struggle with distillation at home make mistakes with this step hence the reason for their struggle.

If you get it right with the process of creating your moonshine mash, you will get the rest of the process right so always pay close attention to the beginning details.

There are different kinds of pulp for moonshine; some purists believe that corn whiskey mash is the best option for a richly-flavored paste.

This belief in the value of corn has made some corn farmers distill their corn to create excellent tasting moonshine for profit. Aside from the corn approach, you can also use the "Sugar shine" approach (that is very popular for beginners).

This sugar shine approach eliminates the corn flavor and creates a unique moonshine taste.

One of the most striking details about moonshine is the fact that you can use a wide array of ingredients to create the final product. This versatility with components has led to the availability of varying moonshine products based on individual preferences.

An interesting approach is the "Hybrid approach" that supports the corn mash with sugar. The added sugar can double your mash production as it is much more convenient while enabling the individual to achieve traditional flavors.

Your creativity can be based on your choice of ingredients (you can always do this much later when you have gotten better with creating the traditional moonshine).

So how do we create moonshine?

Let's find out!

We will begin with the corn mash recipe, and you will need:

Fermentation bucket

A long spoon

Mash pot

Gallons of water (5)

Yeast

Malted barley (crushed, 1.5 pounds)

Heat source

Thermometer

Corn maize (flaked, 8.5 pounds)

The process

Step one

Put the mash pot on your heat source and add the 5 gallons of water. The water should heat up to 165 degrees.

Step Two

Turn off the heat source when it gets to 165 degrees and stir in the 8.5 pounds of flaked corn maize. Continue stirring for some minutes within 30 seconds intervals until the temperature gets to 152 degrees.

Step Three

After the mixtures cool off add the 1.5 pounds of crushed malted barley. Then check to ensure that the temperature is stable (check every 30 seconds).

Step Four

When the mixture cools to 70 degrees, add yeast but please note that it will take some hours before the temperature gets to 70 degrees. You can speed up the process by using an immersion cooler.

Step Five

Ensure to aerate the mixture by placing it in and out of two containers for about 5 minutes. Add the mixture to your fermentation bucket as you are now ready for the fermentation process.

Fermentation

To ferment the mixture, you will need:

Citric acid

Siphon

pH meter (this should be an advanced meter)

hydrometer

cheesecloth

Leave the mash to ferment for about 1-2 weeks (room temperature). The right temperature is critical here because if the room is too cold, it can affect the fermentation process. After all, the yeast will become inactive.

To achieve good results with temperature, you should use a hydrometer to confirm the start of the fermentation process and when it is complete (just to make sure all sugars are used). This means you have to write down the gravity reading when fermentation begins and then the reading at the end of fermentation.

The formula will also help you ascertain the amount of alcohol that will be produced. Next, you have to strain:

The straining process

To strain, all you have to do is siphon the mash water from the mixture. Ensure that you leave all solid materials in a container (this aids the adjustment of pH).

Strain the mash water using a cheesecloth.

At the advanced distilling level, you may add about two tablespoons of gypsum to the mash. Then test the pH of the water because the ideal pH is 8 to 6.0 which means if the pH level is too high you can use citric acid to bring it down and calcium carbonate to increase it.

Well done, you are doing well thus far so let's get on with distillation, shall we? To distill you will need:

Column packing

Moonshine still

Cleaning products

The fermented and strained mash water

First, you have to prep your still for the process by first ensuring it is clean (I know I have repeated this all through this practical section, but it is because it is most important). To avoid a salt build-up that will affect the final product, you must clean your still.

If there is packing to your column, then you should pack it with the right amount of copper that is appropriate for the set-up process. If the setup has a condenser, then ensure to hook the water input and output.

Now you can add your mash water to the still. Use a cheesecloth or an auto-siphon if you've got one) to transfer the mash water to the still (remember to avoid the inclusion of solid materials). You need to try to reduce all sediments in the water to 0%. Next, you have to run your still (that is the fun part of the moonshining process).

Running still is also known as the distillation process, and it entails separating the different chemicals by using different evaporation temperatures. During this process, you are not creating alcohol s you are only separating it from other substances present in the mash water. During the fermentation process, you had already created all the alcohol with the help of the yeast.

Next, bring your temperature to 150 degrees and when you get to this level if you have a condenser turn on the condensing water. Get your heat source to a high level until the still starts to produce. Check the timing for your drips until you achieve 3-5 drips every second. When you get to this level, reduce the heat to maintain a medium setting.

The distillate, level ensures that the drips are getting into a glass container and not a plastic one.

If you use plastic, the product will be laced with BPA, and this will cause several other issues for your health.

Remember to get rid of the foreshots, heads and leave the hearts. You can use the tails later for another distillation process.

With this process, you have succeeded in creating the right moonshine product. Allow the set-up to dry and cool off in a dry place.

With moonshine, in particular, you are working as a scientist that pays specific attention to the process. Some people, learn how to create moonshine the first time and cannot re-create the same great-tasting product because they didn't pay attention to their process.

It is possible to get better with your moonshine production and become an expert, but it is also possible to fail at it the second time.

Sometimes you will love the final product when you try new components and sometimes you wouldn't like it; it is all okay. So long you keep trying, you will surely get better.

The most important thing you need when making moonshine is a suitable container for the mash. Many moonshine makers end up using automotive glass jars because with glass, you can get very high sterilization temperatures as a result of the introduction of copper.

The most commonly used containers are from blue or amber glass.

Depending on the amount of mash that you plan to make, you can start with a smaller amount of mash that will be filled in the largest container. You should avoid using plastic containers. The best bottles for moonshine are those with a cork.

Instead, you can use glasses with wax stoppers. You can also use a stainless steel funnel, copper tubing, and a 3-liter glass container.

You can boil water in the kettle in which you will boil the mash because this will prevent the mash from sticking to the bottom of the container.

To sterilize the glass containers before you start, set them in boiling water for at least 30 seconds.

Although it is best to use a food-grade container, you can also use a container that you are using every day and that needs to go away from you.

The containers that you use for moonshine should be able to hold at least 30 liters of mash.

Do not use a container that is 10-liters.

The mash should be sifted before you place it in the container. Use coarse and medium-sized stainless steel mesh so you can easily remove the mash from the container.

A sterilized jar will be used to store the yeast. It must be a transparent jar so you can see how dark the liquid is.

Use the fine mesh strainer for sterilization so the mash will be cleaned before it is poured into the storage jar. The filter will be used for filtering the mash before it is stored.

Arrange the boiling container as the first filter where the mash is filtered at the beginning of the process.

The grain needs to be washed before you can do it.

Chapter 4: How to Make Whisky

We will begin our practical section with a common alcoholic beverage that is incredibly tasty: *whisky*.

While the whisky you buy at the store is excellent, preparing your unique blend allows you to create a signature drink with the kind of ingredients you desire.

Through this process, you will learn how to make a whisky brand that suits your taste perfectly.

To get gallons (that is 7.6 liters of whisky), you will need:
- A clean pillowcase/clean cheesecloth
- I cup champagne yeast (please check the manufacturer's instructions before using this).
- A burlap sack (large)
- Water (5 gallons which are also 19 liters) you might need more warm water when you get to the sprouting stage. Follow the instructions carefully, and you will know when.
- Whole untreated kernel corn (10 pounds, .5 kg)

We will begin making whisky now.

Step one

The first step entails sprouting the corn and making the base of your whisky, that is the mash. To sprout the kernel corn you have to get it wet and allow the sprouts to grow. After the corn is sprouted, it is ready to be made into a mash. This mash is a combination of grains and warm water, the enzymes inside the mash will break down the starch in the gain, thus producing sugar.

Step two

Put 4.5 kg of untreated kernel corn into a burlap sack and put the sack in a bigger bucket or container. Saturate the burlap sack with water (please use warm water) please make sure the corn soaks evenly as this is crucial for the end product.

Now you may be wondering "Why should I sprout the corn for the whiskey".

Well, you sprout the corn because it eliminates the need for sugar that could have been added to the mash. Without added sugar, you will have a delicious and organic whisky made with the finest ingredients. Sprouting (also referred to as malting) enables enzymes in the corn to convert starch to sugar (the sugar then becomes the foundation of the alcohol in the whisky).

Step three

Allow the kernel corn to sprout for 8-10 days by keeping the bag in the dark, warm space (a basement is an ideal space). Ensure that the corn remains is damp for about seven days and while sprouting keep the corn's temperature between 62 and 86 degrees.

Step four

Now remove the sprouted ends of the corn when it is ¼ inches long/ rinse the corn in clean water and remove the grown roots by hand while discarding the sprouts.

Step five

With a rolling pin, wooden muddler or any other equipment, crush the kernels in the fermenter until they have all been broken apart.

In some cases you can use a grist mill to crack the kernel open, just make sure it dries up properly so it can go through the grist mill.

Step six

Pour 5 gallons of boiling water on the corn mash because at this stage you are ready to ferment.

Step seven

Now you will ferment the mash, but first, you should know that when making whiskey, all instruments and tools MUST be kept clean.

If you work with unclean tools in a polluted environment, the whiskey itself can become contaminated. Contamination can ruin the entire whisky so you must sterilize thermometers, airlocks, containers (and their lids) as well as your hands (do this before you start).

Step eight

Let the mash cool down to about 86 degrees (always use a thermometer to test the temperature). What you want to achieve here is a fresh mash that is also still warm enough for the yeast.

Step nine

Next, put the yeast on the top of the mash, close the lid on the fermenter and leave it for about 4-5 minutes. Then pitch the fermenter to one angle while moving it back and forth (this will agitate the yeast, and cause it to start working).

Step ten

An airlock is crucial for fermentation as it allows CO_2 to escape without air getting to the mash. I air gets into the mash, the effect of the yeast will be affected, and it will ruin the entire process. You can also make an airlock if you don't want to buy one (but it is not an expensive item, so it is advised that you buy one).

Step eleven

The process of fermentation will take 5-10 days (this depends on the temperature, yeast and the amount of grain you use). With the help of a hydrometer, you can confirm when primary fermentation is complete. If the thermometer gives the same reading for more than two days, then distillation can begin.

Remember to keep the mash at a steady level (77 degrees), and while fermenting, you will need heat or the yeast to become active (this will make it consume the starch). After fermentation of the mash strain and siphon it into a still.

To strain the mash, use a clean pillowcase or cheesecloth to keep solids away from the still when transferring the mash.

Now you are ready for distillation.

Distillation process

Step one

The mash that is free from all solids is referred to as either a wash, sour mash, or wart. The wash should have about 15% alcohol in volume and distilling it will increase the alcohol content. To achieve better results, get a pot still.

Step two

Heat the wash slowly until it gets to a boil but remember not to rush the whisky distillation process. Heat the still (medium heat) for 30 minutes to one hour until it boils. If you heat the wash-up too quickly, it will lead to lead to a burnt wort with burnt flavors. The temperature at this time should be at 172 degrees to 212 degrees.

This temperature is ideal because alcohol and water have varying evaporation levels. While alcohol evaporates at 172 degrees, water evaporates at 212 degrees. This realization means that if you heat the wash to 172 degrees band not beyond 212 degrees, the evaporated liquid (inside the still) will be alcohol and not water.

Step three

The condensing tube is meant to take the evaporated alcohol and cool it off quickly, but you have to turn on the tube when the wash is at 120-140 degrees. Gradually, the condensing tube will start to bring forth liquid.

Step four

Throw out the heads. The head is a mix of inconsumable compounds that evaporate into the wash. The compounds include methanol (this is a poisonous compound). The heads usually come out first so for an 18-liter gallon throw away the first 50-100 ml.

Step five

After the heads are gotten out, you will be ready to get the right part. When the thermometer on the condensing tube gets to 175-185 degrees, you can start collecting the valuable part, that is the body of the distillate.

Step six

Remember to throw out the tails which comes out when the thermometer reads 205 degrees. Turn the heat off, so the pot cools down. So what you have now is a high ABV (Alcohol by volume) whisky that may be too harsh for you to drink. For you to get whisky that is close to what you have in stores, you have to dilute it to about 40-50% ABV.

Step Seven

Before you dilute you will want to know the ABV level first and to do this, you can use proof and tralle hydrometer. The readings of the proof and tralle can be confusing so try not to get confused. The poof will be twice the amount of tralle (this is how you get an accurate reading).

Step eight

Now you are ready to age the whisky!

The whisky can go into the barrel when it is at 58-70% ABV, this process makes the whisky smoother and gives it a very rich taste, but the whisky must age in barrels and not in bottles, if you put it in a bottle it will stop aging.

Oak barrels are also the best options; they can be charred or toasted barrels. You can get the barrels from other distillers that have aged whisky in them before. You can ass some toasted oak chips into the barrel, the chips are aromatic and will give the whisky a unique taste.

If you use the oak chips option, you should strain the whisky to remove the chips before consumption after removal put the whisky back in the barrel and allow it steep between 5-15 days (or longer based on your personal preference).

Step nine

You have to dilute the aged whisky before you can bottle or drink it. At this stage, the whisky is about 40-45% ABV which guarantees better taste.

Step ten

Now you can bottle your whisky and drink responsibly :)

Whisky is always a great- tasting alcoholic beverage, but to get a distinctively rich taste, you must follow the instructions and processes carefully.

The final product you get will be worth the entire process, and you will be glad you took on this adventure.

Chapter 5: How to Make Vodka

Vodka is one of the most loved alcoholic beverages, especially by people who like drinking neutral spirits.

Vodka doesn't age, and it is made from fermented fruits, sugars, potatoes, and grains, to produce alcohol. As a homebrewer, you have to be very cautious with the vodka distilling process as you must discard methanol, which can be damaging when consumed.

The fact that you will be distilling at home with minimal or no supervision means you should be extra careful with the entire process.

Pay close attention to the steps you will find below and ensure that you keep your distilling space clean at all times.

Preliminary steps and general information

First, you will have to choose your ingredients (the ones you want to ferment into vodka).

Vodka is commonly made from rye, corn, potatoes, barley, or wheat. You can also use sugar and molasses, which can be added ingredients or used as a stand-alone ingredient. Regardless of what you chose, they must be sugars or starches because this is what produces alcohol.

When you add yeasts with sugar or starch, it births alcohol and carbon dioxide.

If you are making vodka from grains and potatoes, you must create a mash that will contain active enzymes that break down the starch from grains into fermentable sugars. If you are using fruits, then you wouldn't need the paste as fruit juice already contains sugar after fermentation. Wine can be a medium that is distilled into vodka.

You may have to add enzymes based on what you decide to make your vodka from; the enzymes will change the starch to sugar. If you settle for grains and potatoes, you will need more enzymes as these are high sources of starch; as such, they will need enzymes to break down the starch into sugar.

If you chose malted whole grains, then you will not need additional enzymes. Malted barley and wheat are rich in enzymes that break down the starches into fermentable sugars. If you work with refined sugars, then you don't need additional enzymes because sugar is already available.

First, you will need the following:

Ingredients for the base
- Gallons of water (7)
- Thermometer
- Mash pot
- Long spoon
- 25 pounds of potato
- Crushed malted barley (5 pounds)
- Heat source

The mashing procedure

- Start by scrubbing the potatoes with a produce brush (this removes all dirt)
- Cut the potatoes into cubes to increase the surface area
- Boil the potatoes for 20 minutes in 7 gallons of water
- Mash potatoes using an immersion blender or by hand
- Transfer the mash to the mash pot. Add water to reach a total of 7 gallons in volume
- Increase the heat of your paste to 140 degrees, stir the mix continuously until you get the desired temperature.
- Add five pounds of crushed malted barley and stir continuously while adding barley.
-

- Hold the mash at 140 degrees for about 20 minutes and stir for 30 seconds every 4 minutes.
- Increase the temperature to 152 degrees and hold it for 1 hour while stirring for 30 seconds every 10 minutes.
- Read the gravity level if it is below 1.065, add sugar to reach .065.
- Cool the mash to 75 degrees, and if time allows you to cool, you can do so overnight. When kept overnight, the enzymes in the barley have time to break down the potato starch.

Fermenting the potato vodka mash

For this next stage, you will need:
- Yeast
- Siphon
- Citric acid
- Fermentation bucket

- Cheesecloth
- Advanced ph Meter
- Iodine (this is optional)

Fermentation process

Start by creating a yeast using the steps below:

- Sanitize a mason jar
- Pour sanitized water into the jar (it should be 4 oz of 110degree)
- Add two teaspoons of sugar to the water and stir
- Mix the yeast in (the amount depends on the type of yeast you use, always follow the directions).
- Stir the mixture
- Allow the starter to sit for 20 minutes; you will see the volume of the mixture double.
- Transfer the mash liquid to the fermentation bucket. Pour the mash through a strainer to do this and try to aerate the mixture by making a splash, but don't lose liquids.
- Add the yeast starter to the fermentation bucket and add an airlock.
- Ferment the mixture for two weeks at room temperature.
- Use iodine to check if the fermentation is complete by taking a sample of the liquid off the top.
- Place the sample on a white plate or a lid and add a few drops of iodine. Watch the sample closely; if it turns blue, then it means it has reacted completely to the starch. If starch is still present, then it implies fermentation is not complete, so you will have to check again in a few days.

- After fermentation is complete, you will have to remove solid materials as if they are leftovers; they can cause headaches. You can remove such solid materials with cheesecloth as this should be done before distillation.
- Now we are ready for distillation!

The process of distillation

Below are the tools you will need for distilling vodka

- Still
- Cleaning products
- Mash water (fermented and strained)
- Column packing

At this point, you have completed the most significant part of the vodka-making process, but it is not perfect vodka yet.

You have to separate the vodka from other unwanted stuff, and this is the distilling process.

First, you must prepare your still as if you want a great tasting vodka you must ensure that the still is very clean. Add some neat copper packing to your column; if you are working with a condenser, hook up the water and then add your wash to the still. You should use an auto-siphon for this process so you can reduce the amount of sediment.

You have to run your still, so ensure that the column is packed with copper packing. Turn up the heat source and increase the temperature of your wash. If you are working with copper still, apply some flour paste to the joint between the vapor one and column when it reaches 110 degrees. If you are using a condenser, ensure that the water is turned on when the boiler reaches 130 degrees.

At 170 degrees, the still will begin production, and you will want to dial in your heat source to get 1-3 drips every second. The next step will be the collection of your potato vodka distillate.

The most exciting part of this entire process is collecting your vodka.

However, this is where you have to pay even closer attention.

You have to know what to throw out and what to retain, so here is the breakdown:

Throw out the foreshots

The first 5% of the run will be the foreshots that contain methanol (it is volatile and toxic), so please do NOT consume this part of your mix.

If you consume methanol, you can develop some health issues of which blindness is a possibility.

Isolate the foreshots and throw them out.

Get rid of the heads

The next 30% of the vodka is the heads; it is similar to foreshots and also contains volatile alcoholic substances. A significant part of the heads is known as acetone, which has a distinct smell. Although acetone will not make you blind if consumed, it will give you a most terrible hangover. Isolate the heads and throw them out.

Keep the hearts

The next 30% is the hearts, and it is a sweet part of the vodka. The solvent smell of acetone will wear out, and you will perceive the sweet smell of ethanol.

At this point, you know you have succeeded with distilling your vodka, but you will need your sense of smell to be on high alert as to know when to smell the hearts, identify the heads, and see when the foreshots are out.

The tails

The last 35% will be the tails; it contains protein and carbohydrates from the wash you don't need in your product. Ethanol concentration decreases with the tails so you can set the tails aside and use them as wash later.

Congratulations are in order as you have just learned how to make delicious potato vodka.

Don't worry if you have a little variation with your first attempt as with time and consistent repetition; you will get it right.

Also, don't forget to clean up after getting your vodka, wash everything you used, and maintain a neat distilling space.

Chapter 6: How to Make Rum

Unlike other spirits, rum has a much simpler production process, yet the procedures for making rum at home differs from person to person.

Due to the different ways of producing rum that cut across varying cultures, there are different ingredients you can use, but all of them are from one primary source: the sugarcane plant. Rum is made with unsulfured molasses, that is a product one gets from refined sugarcane.

The reason you should use unsulfured molasses is that sulphured molasses contains sulphur oxide (this serves as a preservative).

The process of sulphuring gives the molasses a chemically-infused flavor, and this isn't right for your rum hence the reason for unsulphured molasses.

You can also use raw sugar cane or its juices if you don't have access to molasses.

A lot of rum recipes use unsulphured molasses gotten from sugarcane plants. The molasses flavors are light, blackstrap, and dark (you can get blackstrap molasses for the rum wash).

Making rum, the wash recipe

- Heat source
- Thermometer

- Brew pot
- Raw sugar cane (8 pounds)
- Blackstrap molasses (1 gallon)
- Long spoon
- Rum turbo yeast (the one for professional use)
- Water (6.5 gallons)

The sugar/molasses wash process

Step one

Put your brew pot on the heat source and pour in the 5.5-gallon water.

Step two

Heat the water to 125 degrees and stir in the raw sugar cane and molasses. Stir the mix with a long spoon until it is all dissolved (please note that you may have to stir for a long time until the molasses disappears entirely).

Step three

After the molasses and sugar are dissolved, add 1 gallon of cold water, so the temperature is not too high.

Step four

Check the temperature of the wash regularly (stir at least every 30 seconds of 5 minutes). When the temperature gets to 80 degrees (after several hours but you can speed up the process if you are using an immersion cooler).

Step five

After the wash cools to 80 degrees, add the rum turbo yeast and aerate the wort. You can aerate the wash by placing it in and out of two separate containers for at least 5 minutes).

Step six

Pour the wash in the fermentation bucket, place the cap and airlock it by sealing the fermentation bucket with an airlock. Store in a dark place (at 75 degrees to 80 degrees).

The process of fermenting the rum wash

You will need:

- Cheesecloth
- Citric acid
- Advanced pH meter

The fermentation process for rum that includes molasses is different from the one made with raw sugar cane. The wash is made from fresh sugar cane ferments for 3-7 days, and when it is ready, it will have a sweet taste. The sweet taste is because of the yeast's ability to convert the sugars in the wash. Fermentation is complete when gas doesn't come out of the airlock in the bucket kit.

The process of straining

After fermentation is complete, you have to remove all solid materials, and cheesecloth is ideal for straining. At the advanced level, some distillers test the pH of the wash; first, the pH should be 4.5 to 5.0, and citric can bring it down if it is too high.

Now you are ready to distill your rum.

You will need:
- A still burner
- Fermented and strained rum wash
- Cleaning products
- Easy-to-use siphon
- Hydrometer
- A pot still

You are doing great at this moment as you have done all that's necessary to produce your fermented rum wash.

The rum wash you have now contains unwanted content that should be separated and disposed of, and this is where distillation takes place.

Distillation makes the rum wash purer and concentrated; the process also separates unwanted materials such as acetone, methanol, and acetaldehyde.

First, you must clean your pot still (please do not skip this step as it will determine the quality of your finished product).

Add your rum wash into the still (use a siphon for this step)

Make sure the still is well set up, then turn up the heat source and raise the temperature of your rum wash through two distillations.

At the first stage, you will collect all the distillate (without separating anything, you will separate at the second round of distillation).

If you are working with a condenser, then turn on the water when the boiler gets to 130 degrees.

At 168 degrees, the still will begin its production so you can increase the temperature to continue the production of distillate.

When it measures less than 20%, ABV, stop collecting distillate (you will know this with the help of a hydrometer).

Hold on to the content in the still because you will add it back to the second distillation. This process will contribute immensely to the great flavor of the rum.

With 20% of water dilute the first distillate, stir it well and place it back in the still. Now begin your second stage of distillation.

The next step entails collecting the rum distillate, and it is similar to the way you obtain the distillate of other products. First, discard the foreshots (the first 5%).

Then discard the next 30% (heads) until you get a sweet-smelling aroma. Next, you have to age the rum.

Aging

Aging the rum can be done in different ways, and it is influenced by a variety of factors, as explained below:

The type of barrel

A major factor to consider is the type of barrel; you have to know if it should be a charred barrel or a new one. If you work with a charred barrel, the rum will have a dark and rich flavor, with a new barrel, it will have a lighter taste.

The time the rum is aged

Duration is another crucial factor as the longer you age the rum, the more it will take in more of the flavor of the kind of barrel you use.

The area of production

The area in which you produce the rum also matters; if you create in the tropical climate, the rum will mature faster, and this will be because of the amount of product that is lost to evaporation. Before you start the aging process always distillate to 50%.

As mentioned earlier, you can create several types of rum such as white rum, dark rum, and spiced rum, let's find out how you can get such variations.

Spiced rum

When you are done aging the rum, you can add more flavoring such as spices, vanilla, cinnamon, cloves, nutmeg, etc. at this stage; you can experiment with spices and flavors and get to know what you like more. First, mix the spices in another container and not in the rum barrel.

You have to be certain of the spice you want to use before adding it to the barrel.

Dark rum

In some countries, rum is aged for distillation for at least a year while this isn't required at all times; if you want dark and rich flavored rum, you will have to age it for about 6 -18 months. The aging process for this type of rum has to be in an oak barrel with oak chips that give it a unique flavor.

Regardless of the duration, you chose to age the rum ensure that the blend is consistent when mixing as this is the last step for a good and adequately aged before bottling.

White rum

For the white rum, it is usually very light as such aging is not required; all you to do is dilute the drink with water. When it gets to 45%, you can blend the mix, bottle the spirit, and leave the bottle untouched for about four days.

Within the four day duration, the flavor will stabilize, and this means your rum will age without a dark color.

Chapter 7: Tips and tricks

There are a few things you can do and most are tricks that can help your patience and your end product. I've included these in the following how-to.

Some things to keep in mind before you even start distilling:

Do not use poisonous materials or liquids as some actually DO boil. Some you can smell before distilling is complete, some you will know by smell and taste and some you will not know at all. Be careful.

Keep everything in the right proportions. Most of you probably have a recipe that works for you, but always keep in mind why you picked it to begin with. If you are making rum, you don't want the alcohol to get too high, but too low and you can't use too much sugar or the proof won't come out the same.

So, you're in the middle of a fun experiment and something goes wrong. You have been nice and patient with your batch of moonshine and you have used good quality bottles, only to find out while you are bottling it that your beverage is spoiled. Does it all have to go to waste? Not if you are following these instructions.

Keep your glass bottle (I prefer static free spray paint) for only one thing. Clean it thoroughly after each bottling to avoid build ups. One little spot of mold can ruin a batch and yes, it does hurt. The good news is that when you do end up with some ruined batch, it won't hurt you.

How to Avoid spoilage

Open all bottles of moonshine in a clean place instead of drinking them. Do not drink it. If you use your mouth to open a bottle, don't taste the moonshine, don't do shots of your moonshine, don't even drink it in a shot glass. Gravity will pull the bad stuff down to your stomach. You may not even know it, but it can be permeating your gut and giving you some intestinal problems. As far as I know, it won't hurt you, it may just feel uncomfortable. As long as it stays in your stomach, you will probably be alright.

Keep your yeast in a non medicinal container. You can buy or find a glass jar that has a little lid with a hole in it. This is a perfect storage jar for your yeast. It doesn't leak, it can't break (although the aftermath of broken glass is not good.)

Keep it clean. Don't leave your moonshine sitting out for a day or two. Keep it in the freezer so it doesn't go bad.

The yeast needs water. You will want one cup of water for every cup of beer you have. You can substitute the water with fruit juice if necessary – about a cup of fruit juice per cup of moonshine.

The yeast and water needs to be at room temperature to activate the enzyme in yeast. Sometimes it takes a couple of weeks for the yeast to react. A little wine will do the trick – a few drops of wine in the cup of yeast and water.

The best way to tell if your yeast has reacted is to taste it after about two weeks. If you have tasted it, the yeast should have changed (syrupy) and it should smell like vinegar.

Recipes

Apple Pie Shine

This recipe is stunning and tastes like real apple pie.

Ingredients

- 2 liters apple juice.
- 2 liters cider.
- 2 cinnamon sticks.
- 2 cup sugar.
- 1 Tablespoon honey.
- 1 liter 50% ABV alcohol

Directions

1. Mix the cider, apple juice, sugar, cinnamon sticks and honey into a large pot and place on the stove. Heat until boiling and keep mixing with a spoon.
2. Once it boils switch off the heat and leave to cool down to room temperature. At this point you can add the alcohol.

3. At room temperature you can add the alcohol and mix it thoroughly. You are now ready to bottle this golden nectar. You can add a piece of cinnamon stick to each bottle or even an apple slice if you wish that is your choice.

4. It tastes like the real thing.

Fruit Preserves

Get the fruit that is in season and peel it then cut it up. Place it in big mason jars and pour a 25% ABV mix over it all and seal the jar. Leave it for a few weeks then eat with ice cream. Yummy!

Apple, Plums or Pear slices

Peel the fruit and slice into strips. Make a syrup using sugar and add alcohol at about 18-20% mix. Fill the bottle and seal. Store till needed. A stunning pudding or filler for a trifle.

Colored Drinks

You can make drinks into all colors simply by adding cake coloring as well as flavors using the same flavoring used in cakes. This can be an interesting project for you.

Irish coffee

Make a pot of coffee using either ground coffee or a better make instant.

Whip some cream so it is still slightly fluid and have a teaspoon handy.

Pour the coffee into a wine glass, (make sure it can take the heat), and then put a tot of spirits in the coffee.

Turn the teaspoon upside down and pour the cream slowly over the coffee and it will make a white layer with the black coffee underneath.

Drink the coffee through the cream.

Sweets and Candies

Buy some boiled or jelly candies and place them in a jar. Pour some 20% mix alcohol over them and shake them from time to time. Try to use candies with the same flavor or you will get a real Hodge podge at the ned.

Try using liquorice or mints, in fact you can even try using chocolate as well but all of them must be shaken well to be absorbed into the liquid.

These are all fine for ice cream toppings.

Pickled Alcohol Onions

Try to pickle onions in alcohol, by peeling the small onions, and covering them with salt to dehydrate them. Leave overnight and then wash off all salt. Place in a jar and then mix sugar and pickling spices to the alcohol. This recipe is exactly the same as a vinegar pickle except we use the alcohol for a little extra oomph!

Pickled Macadamia Nuts

Place clean white unblemished nuts in a jar

Dilute a cup of sugar in a small quantity of water and add to a sealable jar.

Put 20% by volume alcohol into the jar and make up the balance with water and two to three drops of white vinegar for tartness (you can ignore this of you do not want this).

Fill the jar to the rim and seal.

Let stand for four weeks or more and then taste.

Liqueur Types

The following list are examples of liqueur types you can make at home.

Advocaat

Apple Schnapps

Apricot Brandy

Blackberry

Black Raspberry

Black Sambuca

Butterscotch

Cappuccino

Caramel / Vanilla

Chocolate Cream

Crème de Menthe

Dry Vermouth

Hazelnut

Irish Cream

Irish Mint Cream

Macadamia

Mango

Melon

Marula

Orange Brandy

Orange Truffle

Pastis

Peach Schnapps

Pina Colada

Red Sambuca

Rum Liqueur

Scotch Heather

Southern Comfort

Strawberry

Swiss Chocolate Almond

White Sambuca

Keep a log of the ingredients for future use.

Banana Liqueur

Ingredients

- 2 x Large Bananas peeled and slices finely.
- 11/2 cups rum
- ½ cup water
- ½ cup brown sugar

Directions

1. Place the bananas in a large bowl or jar that can seal.
2. Add the alcohol.
3. Seal and shake the container.
4. Place in a cool dark place for three days
5. Strain out the pulp.
6. Filter juice through a coffee filter to remove bits of banana.
7. Het the water and sugar mix on medium heat until it boils into a syrup.
8. Mix with the banana juice.
9. Seal in a jar and shake to mix.
10. Leave to settle for one day.
11. Store in a fridge for 2 months

Brandy and Rum Mix Liqueur

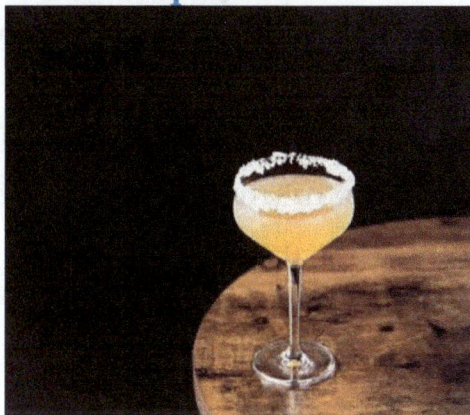

Ingredients

- 750mL Brandy or alcohol with brandy essence.
- 125mL Rum as above
- 6 x cloves
- 1 x Cinnamon Stick
- Half teaspoon ground nutmeg
- Zest of a tangerine
- Syrup Mix
- 200g (1 cup) Sugar
- 125mL (half cup) water

Directions

1. Put the brandy and rum mix into a large jug.
2. Mix the spices, mash them together then add them.
3. Add the tangerine zest.
4. Add the spices and zest, and place into the liquid into the liquid.
5. Place all of the ingredients into a bottle and seal it.
6. Store for one month in a cool dark place.
7. After one month filter out all solids.

8. Make the syrup by placing the water and sugar in a pot and the water has reduced into a syrup form.
9. Mix the syrup and mix and bottle.
10. Leave for a month to age in a cool dark place.
11. Serve on ice cream. Yummy!
12. This mix should make about one liter.

Cherry Brandy

Ingredients

- 4 x Cups cherries washed and de pipped.
- One and a half cups sugar
- 750mL alcohol

Directions

1. Wash and remove stems and pips from the cherries.
2. Mash the fruit.
3. Place in a sealable jar
4. Dissolve the sugar in the alcohol.
5. Cover the fruit with this mix.
6. Seal the jar and store in a cool dark place for six months.
7. Strain the pulp out of the mix using a coffee filter.

Alternative

You can keep the fruit intact.

Remove the skins.

Cover with the alcohol and sugar mix and store for two months.

Use with ice cream or other fruits.

Cointreau

Ingredients

- Zest from 3 small oranges
- 1 x tablespoon bitter whit from an orange
- 1 x cup brandy
- 1 cup vodka
- 4 x Cloves
- 2 x cups sugar
- 1 ½ cups water

Directions

1. Combine the zest and peel to the brandy, vodka, and place in a sealable container.
2. Store in a cool and dark place for 20 days and shake daily.
3. Add the cloves after 20 days.
4. Allow to steep for one day.
5. Boil the sugar and water to make a syrup.
6. Strain the zest mix through a coffee filter to remove bits.
7. Mix both liquids.
8. Store for three months

Coffee Velvet

Ingredients

- 5 ml vanilla extract
- 1 x tin condensed milk
- 500 ml brandy
- 500 ml coffee creamer
- 5 ml instant coffee granules
- 5 ml glycerin
- 1 x large tin evaporated milk

Directions

1. Dissolve coffee granules in warm water.
2. Mix all ingredients together without too much beating.
3. Leave to stand for 24 hours before bottling.
4. Keep refrigerated.

Drambuie

Normally Scotch Whiskey is used but we can use our alcohol products. Johnny Walker Black is the norm, but you can make that using the whiskey kit if you have one.

Ingredients

- 750mL alcohol
- 2 x cups honey
- Quarter teaspoon chopped angelica root.
- Quarter teaspoon fennel seeds
- 1 x full zest of one lemon

Directions

1. Combine all the ingredients together in container that has a sealing lid.
2. Shake every hour for 24 hrs.
3. Remove the lemon zest (tea strainer)
4. Seal and place in a cool dark place for two weeks and shake daily.
5. Remove the angelica and fennel using a tea strainer.
6. Store for 6 months in a dark cool place.
7. Pour into a carafe or bottle and label.

Irish Cream

Ingredients:

- 1 x cup Irish whiskey (i.e. Jameson's)
- 1 x cup Heavy cream
- 1 x tin condensed milk
- 2 x tsp Chocolate syrup

- 1 x tsp Pure vanilla extract
- 1 x tsp almond extract

Kahlua

Ingredients

- 4 x cups of water
- 1 x cup instant coffee (good make)
- 2 x cups light brown sugar
- 2 x cups dark brown sugar
- 750mL alcohol like vodka
- 3 x tea spoons vanilla extract
- 1 x vanilla bean split in half.

Directions

1. Boil the water and add to the coffee.
2. Stir in both of the sugars.
3. Stir and simmer for 3 hours and stir every 20 minutes.
4. When it gets thick remove from the heat and add the alcohol and vanilla's.

5. Seal the bottle and store in a cool place for one month and shake weekly.
6. Split the mix into smaller bottles and place some vanilla in each bottle.

Lemonade Liqueur

Ingredients

- 6 x lemons
- 6 x Cups water
- 2 x cups sugar
- 200mL alcohol

Directions

1. zest the lemons and squeeze the juice out minus the pips.
2. Place in a jug and mix in 2 x cups sugar (any type will do).
3. Add 6 x cups of water and heat until boiling.
4. Allow to cool down to room temperature then a dd 200mL of alcohol (or to taste, your choice).
5. Chill and serve.

Orange and Lemon Aged Liqueurs

Both of these fruits have the same recipe so we offer them both together to save space and time for you.

Clean the fruit thoroughly and allow to dry.

Rasp the color parts (zest) of the fruit into a bowl using a cheese grater or even cut with a small knife, do not use the white parts, as they are bitter.

Place the pieces in a bottle and add sugar and alcohol at 20% mix.

The sugar should be fine like castor sugar for easy mixing, and quantity depends on the fruit used and the size of the bottle used.

Leave the mix for a week, and then strain through a coffee filter to remove the zest pieces.

Rebottle and fill to the top. Seal the bottle (a Mason jar is about the best to use).

Store in a dark cool place for two to three months or until you cannot wait any longer to try it out.

Again keep a record of quantities used and log them.

Sambuca

Ingredients
- 750mL alcohol

- 100g Star Anise
- 25g Elderberries
- 400g Sugar
- 550mL Water

Directions

1. Mix the anise, elderberries and alcohol and then stir it up.
2. Place in a sealable container and store for five days in a cool and dark place
3. Shake daily.
4. Strain of all solids using a coffee filter.
5. Mix the sugar and water and heat until a syrup is formed.
6. Any foam formed must be removed using a spoon.
7. Allow to cool.
8. Mix the syrup with the anise mix.
9. Bottle and seal
10. Store for one month and use

Colors

If you want black Sambuca add liquorice and allow it to dissolve in the liquor.

Any other colors you care to make can be produced using food coloring in small quantities.

Slivovitz

If you look at Slivovitz Plum Brandy, it is made by putting overripe damson plums in a tub and allowing it all to basically rot and ferment. When the fermentation has finished then the mix is strained off and the juice put in the pot still and slivovitz is born. They keep it to mature and use it for holidays and religious festivals.

Ingredients

- 20kg preferably blue plums (but most others will substitute)
- 2kg Sugar (optional)

Directions

1. Wash the plums.
2. Remove the pips as they contain a poisonous compound.
3. Mash them up in a large container
4. You can add sugar if you wish but this is optional.
5. Add hot boiled water and stir.
6. Cover the container with a cloth and allow to cool.
7. Add yeast (although the plums generally have their own yeast).
8. Cover with the cloth and stir twice daily.
9. After one week remove the pulp and discard (they generally feed the pigs this part).
10. Filter the liquid and distil in an alembic still.
11. Discard the initial methanol and bottle the rest.
12. The tails are generally kept in to add other flavors, but that again is your choice.

Plums in Bosnia

Southern Comfort

Ingredients

- 1 x 750mL Alcohol

- 2 x Vanilla Beans
- 2 x Dried Cherries
- 4 x Dried Apricots chopped
- 1 x teaspoon Coriander
- 1 x teaspoon Cloves
- 3 x Cinnamon Sticks
- 1 x teaspoon Pink Peppercorns
- 1 x Anise Pod
- 1 x Quarter Orange minus the white
- 1 x Quarter Lemon minus the white

Directions

1. Add all ingredients into a large sealable container.
2. Let stand for 72 hours.
3. Strain off all solids and store in a dark cool place for one month.

Strawberry or Chocolate Milk Mix

You can buy a strawberry or chocolate milk shake quite cheaply.

Add 200mL alcohol to a liter of the shake you end up with a strawberry liqueur.

You can also buy some Nesquik, and mix that in to thicken it,

Just buy the same flavor of Nesquik as it easy to take the wrong one as the packets look similar, (ask me I did it)

This is a stunning drink for the ladies or on ice cream.

Vodka

If you want to make potato vodka that is one of the traditional types of vodka, then you will need to distill the potatoes.

Ingredients

- 10kg potatoes
- 1kg malted barley (wheat or corn)
- Yeast
- Water

Directions

1. Clean the potatoes and boil them with skins in a pot until soft.
2. Remove the water when cool and filter it.
3. Mash the potatoes thoroughly.
4. Add the water back and top up to 20-23 liters.
5. Add the crushed malted barley.
6. Cook the mix to 150oF (66oC) for two hours.
7. Stir the mix every fifteen minutes.
8. Let it cool down to 80° to 85° F (27° to 29° C).
9. During this time, the barley enzymes break down the starch in the potatoes.
10. Put the yeast in the bucket with the mash and cover with a cloth to prevent insects getting in.
11. Stir twice daily until the yeast has really started to work.
12. Filter out the solids and pour the liquid into a fermenter, and seal with a lid and have an airlock fitted.
13. Take a hydrometer reading.

14. Once the airlock has finished bubbling open the lid and take another hydrometer reading to establish the alcohol content.
15. Distil using an alembic still to keep the flavors in the liquor.
16. Remember to eliminate the methanol content.

Tea Leaves

We recommend the use of used tea leaves as most of the tannin and other nasties have been removed.

Ingredients

- 0.5 kg Used tea leaves.
- 1kg Sugar
- 0.5kg Raisins
- 2 x lemons
- 5 liters (about 1 gallon) Water

Directions

1. Soak the raisins in boiling water and allow to soak and swell.
2. Mash them up completely.
3. Remove the zest from the lemons and then remove the white pith.
4. Slice the lemons thinly, and place in a bowl with the zest.
5. Add the mashed raisins.
6. Add the tea leaves and sugar.
7. Heat the water up and pour into the container.
8. Stir everything.

9. Cover with a cloth until cool.

10. When cool add the yeast and stir gently to mix it in.

11. Cover again.

12. Stir twice a day for a week.

13. Filter out all solids and place the liquid into a carboy jar.

14. Fit an airlock and leave to ferment for approximately a two to three weeks.

15. After clearing, bottle it or drink it as it is very tasty.

The following ingredients are used in the same way as the above recipes.

Apple Wine

Ingredients

- 1kg x apples.
- 1kg sugar.
- 5 liters pure water
- 1 x Wine yeast

Dry Apple Cider

Ingredients

- 20 x Large green Apples chopped up not quarters.
- 2 kg x brown sugar.
- 20 liters boiled water.
- 1 x 100g pkts wine yeast
- 10 x Tea Bags

Directions

1. Boil the water and add the sugar then stir. Boil again while stirring and add the quartered apples. Stir for five minutes. Add the tea bags once the temperature has reached 30o Celsius. Stir in the bags to get the tea mix in.

2. Cover with a cloth for two hours then add the yeast. Cover with a cloth to keep vinegar fly at bay. Cover with a lid and airlock for three days. Remove all solids using a sieve and then filter out the small solids using a clean cloth filter. You can squeeze the cloth to get the final amount of liquid out of the fruit and bags using a cloth. Pour back in the bucket and cover until the fermentation is completed. Bottle the cider and allow to settle until clear, then siphon out and rebottle in 5 liter bottles. Once all of the cider has cleared then bottle in half liter to 1 x liter bottles. If you want fizz on opening use about 1 quarter spoon sugar in each liter bottle and shake it until mixed but be careful of explosions. The cider tastes just as nice without it once cooled and is very refreshing. You should get about 5% alcohol from it.

Frequently asked questions

This last chapter of this first section will be on some frequently asked questions (FAQs) that home distillers ask to gain clarity of the process.

Questions are essential because they help shed more light on aspects of creating a unique alcoholic beverage. The answers to the questions will help you make the right decisions and also cause you to understand why certain things happen while creating your homemade wine.

Now when you get to part two of this book (the practical section), you will unravel a wide array of recipes for different beverages. This realization is the reason why the questions and answers you will find below, will cut across different types of alcoholic drinks and aspects of our discourse thus far,

This is an opportunity for you to get answers to some of the questions you may have.

How can I ascertain the strength of my homemade alcohol?

You can do this with the help of an alcometer that is a device with a scale on it that measures alcoholic content. If there is a higher concentration of alcohol, the density of the liquid will be lighter, and the alcometer will sink to the bottom. Then you can read the scale to know the amount of alcohol present, and this will also help you dilute the mixture correctly.

Can I use aluminum still instead of copper still (would it affect the end product?)

Some people use aluminum stills, but you should know that it can become very messy. With aluminum stills, a lot of cleaning is required, and your alcohol will have a metallic smell that may be unpleasant. So if you can stick with the copper still.

How long does it take before I can ferment the wine?

The duration varies based on certain factors such as the kind of yeast you use, the amount of sugar in the wine and even the temperature. While some wine takes up to two or four weeks to ferment, others may take additional time.

What is the best kind of thermometer to use for distillation at home?

To check the temperature inside the still, you can use any kind of thermometer that can go from 100-300 degrees. But when preparing the mash (that is the base of almost all types of alcoholic beverage), you will need a standard thermometer meant solely for pulps. The mash thermometer should be within the range of 32-150 degrees.

What's the quantity of alcohol to be thrown away from the batches I make?

Due to the risk of methanol in the liquid, you must pay close attention to the quantity you should throw out, and this is usually the liquid that comes first. Always throw away the first 50 ml with every production.

Where can I buy the tools and equipment I need to distill at home?

You can get all you need at online stores such as eBay and Amazon. You can also make purchases from stores in your environment.

Can I dilute the wine I make with water?

Of course, you can dilute the wine with water. But this is based on individual preferences, taste the wine first and decide if you want to dilute it or not.

Can I use any kind of yeast for this process?

Different kinds of yeasts offer varying flavors, but brewer's yeast is the best option because it gives the alcoholic beverage a better taste than regular yeast. Always ask questions at your local brewery or supply stores to understand the various kinds of yeast (if you seek other alternatives).

What are the critical things that affect the quality of my final product?

Your choice of stills

You can use a pot still which collects the condensate from boiling and condenses it. You can also use a reflex still which has a different chamber that purifies the condensate before condensing it. Regardless of your choice of still if you follow the directions carefully, you will get a great product.

Alcohol percentage

The last result you get on the rate of alcohol is also an essential factor in determining the quality of the product.

The type of wash

To get the best quality, you must use very high-quality yeast that helps maintain the right temperature for fermentation. If you distil unwanted spirit and do it excessively, you will end up with a poorly created product. Your wash should also contain the best of other ingredients needed to make the right product.

Storing and the ageing process

Storing your product in a cool dark place will help produce a burst of flavors with your drink. While some home-distillers use oak barrels to store their products, some others also add oak chips to the spirit, and this can give a fantastic finished product.

The kind of carbon treatment

Always stick to a reputable brand for carbon that is made specifically for creating such a product.

How many liters of homemade alcohol can I store in my home?

Well, it depends on the alcohol laws in your local community or country. For example, in the USA, you cannot have non-taxed liquor in your home, and the same rule applies to some Western-European countries as well.

In some countries like Britain and the Netherlands, you can produce only a specific quantity of alcohol, and you will be breaking the law if you exceed the amount. With this question, I will advise that you understand the law concerning alcohol creation in your country and abide by it.

What if my homemade wine has a bad smell or taste? What did I do wrong?

Well, the wine could have an offensive sulphur smell (mostly like that of rotten eggs) for varying reasons. The first reason is that your production kit may be unsuitable for the process. The second reason could be that you used too much of a particular ingredient which affects the product. The third reason could be because the batch is contaminated (this happens when equipment is not adequately sterilized) when bacteria sets in, it affects the fermentation process.

Can whisky be diluted with ice?

Yes, you can dilute your homemade whisky with ice. When the ice melts the ABV reduces, and this reduces the high concentration in the liquid.

Is it safe to make my spirits? Is it legal?

Distilling alcohol at home is not allowed in some countries. In countries such as Austria, New Zealand, Russia, Romania, Ukraine etc. it is legal to distill a home. But in some other countries, there might be an outright ban on production or a restriction on the amount to be produced. If you are caught producing alcohol at home when it is illegal in your country, you will be breaking the law. In some countries and cities, you will need to get a license first.

When distilling wine can I use any kind of wine as an added ingredient?

Yes, you can use scraps of wine as you will solely be taking out the alcohol. Even if the wine is dusty, the distilled product will still be useful.

Where can I get an airlock?

Airlocks are easy to get in stores and online as well. More so, you can make one for yourself as it is a prevalent household item.

Can I create moonshine without an ageing process?

A lot of people leave the spirit as it is after creating it without allowing it age. It depends on your personal taste; you may want to age because you want a peculiar taste, and you may not want to as well (work with what you prefer).

Is it natural to make my alcoholic beverage?

It is natural to make your alcoholic beverage at home. In time past (hundreds of years ago, people made their spirits without government regulations). So it is reasonable to desire such a homemade product, but we live in a different time now where there are laws for such things so you must be careful.

Why is my homemade brandy colorless and the one I bought at the store has color?

The reason for the difference in color is ageing. Brandy that ages in wooden barrels or with additions such as honeycombs and wood spirals affect the flavors. These additions also have an impact on the color. If you didn't age your brandy, the color would still be bright, unlike those in the store made by professionals who age for a long time.

The questions above were arranged in no particular order, and I hope the answers you read helped you understand the process even more.

With this section, we have come to the end of part one (the theoretical aspect of our journey). It is time for you to apply all you've just read in section two by taking a more practical approach towards the learning experience.

Get your aprons ready as you are about to create the most amazing alcoholic beverages in your home.

The Lost Handbook of Artisanal Brewing

An illustrated Guide for Easy Homemade Wines, Beers, Meads and Ciders (Tips and Tricks on a budget)

Don Pablo

Disclaimer and Terms of Use: Effort has been made to ensure that the information in this book is accurate and complete, however, the author and the publisher do not warrant the accuracy of the information, text and graphics contained within the book due to the rapidly changing nature of science, research, known and unknown facts and internet.

Table of Contents

Introduction

The unifying theme of this handbook is the use of fruit in the process of fermentation. With the availability of such numerous fruit varieties, we are given an almost inexhaustible supply of fermentable and a few very versatile core yeasts and bacteria. With these components, we can make an almost infinite number of fermentable with the most basic of technical knowledge and gear.

This work is done in the interest of helping you make your unique, and very likely superior, beverages quickly, cheaply, with a minimum of equipment, and with a minimal investment in time. By choosing your ingredients, you will control the flavors you wish to impart to your beverages; for some, the most desirable characteristic of a beverage is its flavor, rather than its strength. This notion comes from a largely puritanical approach to drinking; you will be able to make your decisions about your drinking. Beers flavored with berries might taste better than those made with barleys, or with special grains.

You should keep in mind that control over flavor is only one advantage you will enjoy when you make your beverages. There are no additives, or potential adverse flavorings, in home-made libations. Leave out the chemicals. Leave out the hazardous waste (noting that it is both safe and common to add a non-hazardous small quantity of activated charcoal to clear the beverage of any wild yeast or bacteria). Leave out the media, and keep out the GMO's, chemicals, and pesticides. Go for an organic approach instead. This means that your beverage will be much less acidic and almost certainly higher in antioxidants than any commercially available drink. An added benefit is that your beverage will probably be allergen- free. You will be able to remove all of these to your palate, or your preferences.

Complete fermentation is fermentation with no sugar added. We will be able to make many things in this area, but the most basic flavors will come from yeast (or bacteria) and fruit concentrates. Some ideas will come from experts, or more experienced brewers; others will be our ideas or suggestions from our experience in making something in this field. Some of what we will offer are first, second, and third thoughts on making this or that beverage; these will be preceded by the name of the beverage in question, and the author's first reaction to the subject of the beverage.

Once we have made our beverages, we will move on to an area where we can if you want to add sugar or honey once the fermentation is complete. These will be a cornucopia of things to make, things that cannot be made without the addition of sugar (and other things) to increase the alcohol content of fruit to beyond a level where it can ferment beyond 4% or 5% alcohol by volume. These are topics for individual experimentation in the area of winemaking as we know it. Some may be familiar. Some will probably be unknown to you or even thought of as 'coffee tables' items.

We will travel through the brewing process, from how to mix the water to recipes for a few very simple 'lagers'. We will move from there to ales and even a few beers that we will not be able to make with the methods laid out here. Perhaps you will be able to make higher-alcohol ales, lager ales, and porters, using wild fermentation and your yeast and bacteria from a brewing culture we have compiled, in the fruit culture section.

Chapter 1: Fermentation

Homemade, fresh, unfiltered, unhomogenized, unpasteurized, unsterilized, organic. Whatever is your favorite homebrew beverage, this guide will provide you with the know-how to make it. The book is so complete, it shows you how to make your very own concentrated yeast starters to ensure vigorous and potent fermentations. The illustrated guide resembles a modern "Joy of Cooking," but about beer, wine, and beverage brewing. All the instructions are given in simple, with detailed explanations and recipes. If you're a skillful brewer, then this book can be used as an excellent reference to further your expertise in the art of brewing.

The process of fermentation

Having a good knowledge of the fermentation process is very important because this is what helps you with the winemaking procedure.

Now if you have a detailed and perfect recipe, you may not need extra information on how to ferment, but it is always advisable that you know how to works so you can get it right at all times.

Wine fermentation happens when the yeast consumes sugar and converts it to half alcohol and half CO_2 gas (which is the process of carbonation).

So for example, if you have 5 gallons of juice with 10 pounds of sugar inside, you will ferment the sugar with yeast and have about 5 pounds of alcohol.

The remaining 5 pounds of sugar will become CO_2 so that the batch will be 5 pounds lighter.

The fermentation process also happens in two stages:

The primary fermentation stage (sometimes called aerobic fermentation)

The secondary fermentation stage (also known as anaerobic fermentation)

The primary fermentation

This type of fermentation lasts for 3-5 days and 70% of the fermentation activity happens in these first days. In some cases, you will observe foaming during the time of increasing fermentation.

This primary fermentation is also known as aerobic fermentation because the vessel used for the process is allowed to remain open.

The air that goes into the vessel helps multiple the yeast. Alcohol will be produced during fermentation, but a more significant part of the yeast will also reproduce itself.

The Secondary fermentation

This process happens when the remaining 30% of fermentation activity happens.

Unlike the primary process where fermentation happens within five days, fermentation with this approach lasts for about two weeks.

Secondary fermentation takes more time as it has less activity with each day that passes. You can also attach an airlock to the vessel at this time to reduce the inflow of air.

This reduction in airflow makes the yeast forget about multiplication and gives energy to making alcohol.

However, you should know that secondary fermentation is NOT a second fermentation process (this term is usually confusing for a lot of people).

Second fermentation happens when the excess sugar that wasn't consumed by the yeast restarts fermentation. This situation occurs when a wine is sweetened again before all the yeast is used up.

Sometimes second fermentation happens by accident except for sparkling wines. Sparkling wines are meant to be bottled before the yeast loses flavor.

But aside from the types of fermentation processes, you should also know some important considerations that make the process successful.

Temperature

Temperature plays a crucial role in fermentation because if it is too cold, the yeast will not enable fermentation quickly, and this makes the yeast dormant. If the temperature is too warm, the yeast will ferment just fine, but the flavor will be negatively affected.

The best kind of temperature for fermentation is 72 degrees (you can also use between 70-75 degrees).

Chapter 2: Brewing Materials

They are important , but you won't use all of them in your first few batches. You'll discover when to use them as you experiment and find your favorite styles.

Yeast

The easiest way to start is with active dry (liquid) yeast. I'll go over the importance of yeast selection later in this guide, but for now it's important to use a proven, very reliable strain.

Other things you'll want with your starter after your first few brews

It's best to clamp your bucket to a faucet and pour a small amount of warm water into the yeast and mix it up.

Balancing and Control

Having a good idea of your water pH is a must. It's important to have good control over your brewing process so you can avoid issues and problems before they occur.

Soils and Metals

You are going to want a "buffer" for your soil. I recommend a sponge of some sort.

Sometimes the metal flavor from the brewing bucket can be a bit uninviting to some. You want to protect yourself from this flavor. A wool blanket, a rag, or any other material that you can find to soak up the metal flavor works well.

Having something in place to prevent oxidation after fermenting and racking off is also a good idea.

Yeast and What NOT to Do

Common questions that you might have right at the start of your brewing venture so you can refine your process and get the best results.

The different types of yeasts are classified by how they function when mixed with fermentable sugars. The must is the mix of water, sugar, and fruit or vegetables that we ferment into wine. Sometimes the must is also referred to as a "wort". This is the substance we ferment into beer. The must is also referred to as a "fermentable substance", so I'll use "must" to cover all three terms.

"Safale" yeast is the least aggressive of the types of commercially available yeast. It is what we'd call a top fermenter, meaning it starts working the day after your yeast is mixed in the must. It is commonly used in ales. It is not full of flavor (always more malt character) and it doesn't cause the wort to bubble up. It is often used in white wines. It is the least likely of the more popular yeasts to produce a "smell" as it ferments. It is also probably rated as one of the "less" picky types of yeast some people have.

The "Super High Gravity" yeast and "High Gravity" yeast are also full of flavor, so the flavor from both may be perceived in your finished product. They also will bubble up the wort, so you need to be careful what kind you use. The flavor in these yeasts will also be slightly more complex than Safale, as you'll have an additional layer of flavor above the malt character. There is also a higher potential for the yeasts to collect sediments during the time between when you pitch the yeast and when you get the chance to drink it!

You can also have a strain known as a "Saflager" that is known to produce less acetic acid, which is a flavor that can make it back into the finished beverage when it's consumed.

For cider and other fruit wines, the "grainsy" flavors of these yeasts can be quite good for producing refreshing ciders.

Yeast Viability

When you prepared the Must to pitch your yeast, you should have measured its volume. In the best case, this measurement should have been 11/2 times the volume of you must container. Yeast is viable because once you pitch it to you must it will need to immediately begin fermentation to produce alcohol.

Use a 16 oz. container as a place to scoop up some of the must and then you can add the yeast to the must.

Whatever you do, don't add extra sugar after the yeast is mixed in. This can throw off the nutrients the yeast uses and kill the yeast.

Yeast Herxing

A good, healthy yeast has most likely just grown for its short amount of time and most of it is being used to ferment you must so you may find there is a low amount of dissolved oxygen in your wort.

If you have an insufficient amount of dissolved oxygen in the wort that is fermenting, bacteria in the air can metabolize some of the available sugars in the wort and then produce acetic acid (vinegar). This is harmful to you must and will give it a smell that is off-putting to some.

Another possibility could be that the yeast you used isn't very good. Like I said above, most commercial yeasts are fine for most of us, but it's good to know that you can not only avoid this situation but also detect and remediate it before it ruins an entire batch of the must.

Most commercial yeasts are dead by the time you get your hands on them, but not all of them are. In this way, the yeast will cull the bacteria from your must. It is possible to use a wild yeast if you have access to a large enough quantity of it, or you can simply add a weak anti-bacterial, hopefully lactobacillus bacterial culture.

Keys to Success

Approximately 1 – 2 days after you started your brewing process you should have 1 – 2 inches of vigorously bubbling wort. Aerating your wort is important for the yeast to survive and grow.

The amount of yeast you use per pound of fresh must will determine your fermentation rate. If you have a large amount of yeast per pound of must, then you may find that your fermentation takes more time than desired. A stronger strain of yeast may be a better choice. If you use a weak strain of yeast, you may find your fermentation is fast, but the finished product is with very little aroma or taste.

If you have an insufficient amount of dissolved oxygen in your wort, that could affect your fermentation rates.

Vacuum packing your wort will help preserve your yeast and prevent oxygen exchange.

Stirring the wort helps move oxygen in and out of the wort.

Don't brew during the hottest days of the year.

Chapter 3: The Techniques of Brewing (Artisanal Not Mass Produced)

This is a practical hands-on manual on how to create your wines, beers, meads, and ciders.

It offers a clear explanation of the beer brewing process. It explains procedures of making natural beer starters like home-made fruit and berry yeast starters.

The Artisanal beer brewing handbook is a must-have for beer lovers and wine drinkers. It will also appeal to those who seek a healthier lifestyle in drinking fermented drinks like meads and ciders.

The handbook has been written for those who prefer to prepare their food, wines and alcoholic drinks. It covers various types of fermented beverages such as wine, cider, mead and similar beverages. Refreshing the taste of your favorite drink with purely natural flavors created from home brewing.

Do not follow the directions on ingredient labels. Some of them are downright bizarre. Understand what you're doing before you do it.

2. Watch someone else brew a batch, from boiling to bottling if possible. You may see some bad habits, along with the good. But you'll be a lot more confident that YOU can do it, once you watch the actual process. If you don't have any friends that homebrew, do a google search for a local homebrew club.

3. Get a second opinion. Compare answers to brewing questions from different sources. Don't be afraid or embarrassed to ask for help.

Every brewer started as a beginner and no one starts out knowing everything. If you have a doubt or question, ask someone with more experience for help. Most brewers are more than happy to help. They remember being where you are.

Search the web; ask on forums; consult different books; ask homebrew storeowners. You'll get conflicting answers, but you might also get a consensus. No brewer can know everything and everyone's experiences are different.

4. There are advantages to ordering brewing supplies online, but you need to find a good, reliable local homebrew supply shop too. At times you will need to smell and taste ingredients. You need to have a source of the freshest ingredients possible.

You will need emergency ingredients, or ingredients on the fly. And you will need access to more experienced brains to pick. Use google to find a local homebrew club and ask its members to recommend *their* favorite homebrew supply shop.

5. If you are going to be a homebrewer, you'd better become reconciled with becoming a janitor too. 80-90% of your activity as a homebrewer is cleaning – cleaning, sanitizing, cleaning up after, and sanitizing again. If you're not willing to put the time and effort into doing it right and thoroughly, you might as well start looking for a different hobby right now.

6. Before you start on brew day, especially if you are short on space, categorize, organize and line up all your equipment and ingredients ahead of time. Write out a checklist and schedule for your chosen recipe.

If you prep, prep, prep and organize everything ahead of time, you won't go through any crazed, last-minute hunts for something you needed five minutes ago. The whole operation will be simpler, more relaxed and much more fun.

7. Never rush. You can easily pop the airlock seal off the fermenter lid by accident and drop it into the murky soup of your latest batch, if you are hurrying to finish the last task of brew day.

8. Purposely go out and taste-test a wide variety of beers and take notes about your observations. It will increase your confidence in your level of success and increase your understanding of the elements of beer you like the most and most want to recreate.

9. Start slow and small. Buy a good equipment starter kit for $150-200 and experiment for a while. Don't invest in an expensive automated system. Their purpose is to eliminate variables and produce predictable, consistent results.

But when you are just starting, variables and mistakes are what teach you. You'll know when it's time to upgrade and you'll understand the value of the upgrade better if you relax and enjoy the journey first.

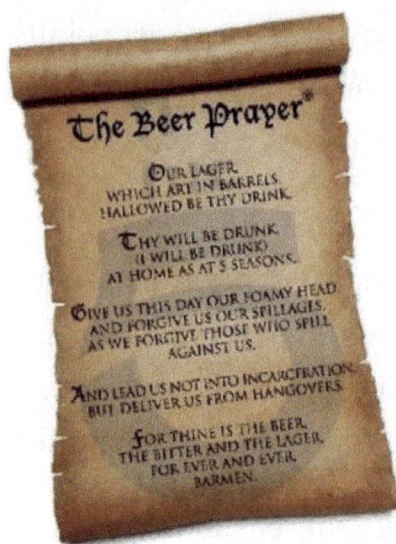

10. Experiment, experiment, experiment. Even if you have a tried and true favorite recipe does not mean it can't be improved. Try a twist or tweak. Switch some hops, or their timing; change some grain; try dry hopping; switch yeasts. I tried an herbal beer for the first time last year. And it was great!

11. Don't ask other brewers if a recipe sounds good. If they never made it they can't know if it's good, and neither can you. I was repeatedly told not to boil fruit for my beer. But I tried it anyway and the resulting beer was a hit. I had pretty much the same experience with my herbal beer recipe. If you experiment and like the result, why seek anyone else's approval?

12. Don't sweat the small stuff. Don't worry if the temperature is off by a degree or two, or the hydrometer reading is off by up to .002.

The only ingredient you need to be really careful about measuring accurately is your priming sugar. And you only need to worry about adding too much, not about adding too little. Too much may cause your bottles to explode. This is supposed to be a fun hobby, not quantum physics.

13. If you make a mistake and realize it too late, don't throw out the batch. If you dump it without tasting it, you might as well flush money down the toilet. Just because you THINK a batch is bad, you can't KNOW it is without tasting it.

Even if you taste the brew, after you realize your mistake, and don't like it, finish the brewing process anyway. Ferment, bottle and age the beer and taste it again. The last stages of fermentation and aging can hugely change and improve beer.

I once fermented a wheat beer at 80°F (27°C) by mistake and it turned out to be one of my best brews ever.

14. Don't demand perfection from yourself every time. If you aren't willing to take chances, including the chance of failure, you won't learn anything and you'll never discover something fantastic and unexpected.

Accept that eventually you will have to throw a batch out and you will relax and enjoy the brewing experience more. Just be careful to take good, complete notes, or you won't learn from either your happy surprises or your unhappy ones.

15. Remember to have fun. Don't get too focused on all the cleaning, the details of numbers, times, charts, recipes, and the waiting for fermentation to start or finish. Remember that you got into this originally for the fun.

Whatever your "real job" is, I'll bet women, and other people, would be far more interested in hearing about making beer than in the details of your "profession". Learn about the differences in beer styles – what makes them different and how different yeasts, hops and grains work together to make them different.

Have fun showing off your knowledge. You'll find it will get you more attention than your "job" does.

16. The best homebrewing advice of all is simply to **relax**. Although there are a great many mistakes you can make, 95% of them will simply result in decent beer, rather than superb beer. No death or dismemberment. It's just beer – not rocket surgery.

Types of distilling methods

Although you will be distilling on a small scale level at home, you must know the significant kinds of distilling techniques. Distilling is an aspect of wine/spirit production that remains constant even when recipes change (you must distil).

So in this chapter, you will learn more about the techniques.

If you visit a modern distillery, you will find very tall columns that are connected by a network of tubes. You will also find squat pots and pumps that aid the production of some of your favourite wine. Distillation is mostly related to the ancient process of alchemy, but it is also simpler than alchemy: the basic idea for distillation is creating alcohol from a lower base.

So one may wonder "Why can' winemakers ferment their mixtures to a higher level instead of distilling?"

Well, the answer lies within the use of yeast in the process. When yeast eats up the sugar (which happens to make beer, spirits, wine, etc.), it creates alcohol, CO_2 and other waste products. However, if more alcohol and CO_2 is created, there will be less sugar for the yeast, and at some point, the alcohol will become too toxic for the yeast.

For us to strike a balance with this process and to get a high ABV level, we must separate the alcohol from water through evaporation and the process of condensation (which is the essence of distillation). Due to its lower boiling point than water (alcohol), the winemakers can evaporate the alcohol, collect vapour into the tube and with cold temperature force the alcohol to condense into a liquid.

Methods of distillation

There are generally two methods of distillation, and other forms originate from these two:

The Alembic method

(which is also known as the pit distilling method)

The alembic method is one of the oldest means of distillation (It was first used in alchemy).

Alembic is a big vessel (like the shape of a kettle), and the wash is heated inside. While heating up ethanol evaporates before the water, the liquid then travels into a cooling tube and into another vessel to condense.

With less water present the ABV will be higher, but aside from the ethanol there will also be other compounds such as methanol, tannis etc. these compounds also have to evaporate during distillation because their continuous presence in the liquid will affect the flavor.

Distillation is meant to ensure that the winemaker gets the right amount of alcohol and all flavoring compounds into the finished product.

The column distilling method

This method became famous as a result of the success of the pot distilling method. As we advanced into the modern world, a lot of commercial distillers started to seek out very easy and faster means of distilling their products. With the alembic method, they had to wash the pot stills after each batch of wine which was time-consuming.

So the column distilling technique is a solution to that problem as it entails the use of giant columns. With this technique, the mash is injected into the column, and the steam can be easily set at the right temperature.

All undesired compounds are left behind, and this method also doesn't require much cleaning like the first one. Repeated distillation processes are possible with this technique, and it is mostly used by commercial brewers who make large batches of wine.

In addition to these top two distillation techniques, there are other forms of distillation that draw inspiration from these two or use their tools and processes to achieve results.

Some of them include:

Fractional distillation

With fractional distillation, alcohol is repeatedly purified to remove water and unwanted elements. Typically, a fermentation mix contains water and ethyl alcohol with a small amount of compounds that make up the flavor of the final product.

The stills used in the fractional distillation process have a multi-column rectifying system that will release pure distillate (with a minimal amount of unwanted elements). To understand this technique well enough, we have to juxtapose it with the simple distillation technique so you can understand how it differs from it and what makes this method unique.

This technique is a modified version of the simple distillation process which separates complex solutions into varying compounds through their different boiling points.

With the simple distillation method, the distillate you get will have a higher level of alcoholic concentration, but water will still be in the mix.

So what you can do is to re-distil to gain a higher alcoholic concentration level. What fractional distillation does is to improve on this simple method by performing the multiple distillations once. The distillation can happen once because of the kind of column used, which is crafted based on how the process occurs.

Another distinction between this process and the simple one is that with simple distillation the vapours from the boiling liquid rises to a column and as the temperature at the height of the column decreases the elements in the mixture will be less volatile. Then condensation takes place in another column (the columns re few centimetres apart).

The second distillation happens with the simple method as the vapours rise and bubble up to the condenser plates. The vapours are then cleaned and purified, but with the fractional distillation, method winemakers can achieve both processes at the same time.

Continuous distillation

This kind of distillation process aims at ensuring continuous operations with winemaking.

The liquid is fed into a still column (it is inspired by the column method) and an equal amount of liquid consistently exists as the mixture distillates. With continuous distillation, professional distillers will not have to empty the still and reload it every time they want a new batch which means it is a more efficient distillation process.

Continuous distillation is also a continuous process with which distillates can flow at a high output level. While this is going on the raw materials for making the wine can be fed into the still at some point without interrupting the collection of finished products.

With the older forms of distillation, the still must be emptied to reload, and this makes the distillation process tiring. The fact that this process is uninterrupted makes it one of the ideal options for distillation.

Although as a beginner and homemade winemaker, you may not have to use this process just yet.

Steam distillation

The steam distillation technique distils alcohol by passing steam gotten from the pot still through plant material. This method is easily controlled, and it is a distillation process that gives the assurance of better quality alcohol as a finished product. The process entails the placement of fresh botanical material in the plant inside the still, and then it is pressurized.

While under pressure, the steam is generated in another chamber in the still and passes through the organic material to remove all oils.

As the steam passes the organic material, the essential compounds of the mixture will be released. The distillate that contains a mix of water vapour and other elements will return to its liquid form after its condensed.

This steam technique is the same process as the simple distillation method as the slight difference between both ideas is the use of steam. When you sue steam distillation for alcohol, you will be retaining the delicate flavors, essence and aromas of the mixture that would have been broken down if it is exposed to a higher temperature.

The steam distillation process is the most preferred method used in the production of Gin because it aids the retention of flavors from aromatic plants. Alcohol can also be made from fermented properties that are placed on the column of the alembic still (a good example is leftover pressed grape skins).

Regardless of how you are distilling your alcohol always remember that alcohol never evaporates alone. Other compounds such as fusel alcohols, methanol and esters can evaporate with it. The idea of "Cutting" is the term used to describe the separation of these other elements through temperature and proper timing.

For example, methanol evaporates at 148.5F, so a winemaker can assert that any liquid that shows up before 173 F should be thrown out. With this example, you can understand that precision is crucial for all distillers because it enables you to focus on the tiniest details that make a difference with the final product.

Distillation has to be done right at all times for you to get the perfect blend and the techniques are crucial.

In this chapter, you discovered some of the essential distillation techniques. Now you understanding of the subject matter has increased but we still have to build on the information you've received.

We are still building on the foundational and theoretical aspect of the book, so in the next chapter, we will focus more on distilling equipment and what you will purchase while preparing for your winemaking process.

Chapter 4: Special Brews : Brewing With Fruit

Fruit: Generally Speaking

Historically fruit has been a popular brewing ingredient. As far back as the Sumerians, brewers were using dates to provide extra sugar and flavor for their beer. Wheat beer, and other bland base beers, can be given a dominant flavor by the addition of fruit.

Fruit can also be used to enhance character by adding a background note. For example, oranges can be used to pump up the citrusy hops of a pale ale.

There are a number of styles of beer that work well with the addition of fruit. Wheat beers are often used as the bases for just about any fruit you can think of. Fruit is also often added to stouts, imperial stouts and porters.

The fruits that can be used for brewing include cherries, citrus fruits, raspberries, blackberries, blueberries, mango, pineapples, apricots, apples, and bananas. Some of them should be made with fruit extract though, rather than with the actual fruit.

Buy your fruit in season at a local farmer's market. Sometimes you can cut a deal because you'll be buying in brewing quantities.

Experiment with the amount of fruit you use. When using frozen or fresh fruit you will need pounds of fruit per gallon of beer.

If you don't like fruit haze in your fruit brews, invest in a small bottle of liquid pectinase or powdered pectic enzyme. It attacks pectin, the carbohydrate in fruit that allows them to thicken jellies and causes haze in fruit beers. However, many fruits that are popular for brewing, such as berries, don't have enough pectin to worry about.

Even when done in a secondary fermenter, the fermentation of fruit can be explosively violent. Use a fermentation bucket or a 6-gallon (23 L) carboy to provide extra room. Also use a blow-off tube rather than an airlock or bubbler. And put your fermenter into a catch basin to make foam-overs less of a headache to clean up.

Fresh, Frozen, Peels, Purees, Syrups, Extracts...

Some types of fruit should be fresh if used for brewing. Citrus fruits are in this category. In the case of citrus fruits, use the peel for its oil. In the case of other fruits, mash them or put them through a blender or juicer to release the sugars.

Many fruits, such as berries, work better for brewing if they are frozen first. Freezing creates crystals of ice that break down the fruit's cell walls and release the juice and sugar. Freeze fresh berries before you brew with them. Keep in mind that freezing does NOT sanitize, sterilize or pasteurize your fruit.

Some fruits and peels work well if added late in the boil. You only need a few teaspoons of citrus oils, while other types of fruit require a substantially greater quantity and soaking time to permeate your beer.

You'll probably be able to find large cans of fruit puree in your local homebrew store. Don't use "pie filling" or any purees that contain other ingredients besides pure fruit. And don't use any that contain preservatives, which can damage your yeast.

When using syrup, puree or juice, add them to your secondary fermenter. If you add them to your primary fermenter, the vigorously produced CO_2 will carry off the fruit aroma as it escapes.

Real fruit makes the best fruit beer. But if it's too expensive, fruit extract is considerably cheaper. But be careful, because some brands will make perfectly awful fruit beer. I recommend Cellar Pro.

Some unusual fruits may only be available for brewing as extracts. Many of these have strong medicinal flavors. They are usually only used in the stronger beers that can mask this off-flavor.

When and How to Use It

If you are making a fruit beer, freeze your fruit first. Freezing ruptures the fruit's cell walls and causes more juice to flow, increasing the fruit flavor in your beer. This is the same reason why you don't want to freeze yeast without adding glycol to it. Refrigeration is usually cool enough for yeast storage.

If you are adding fruit to your beer during the boiling step, mash up your fruit or run it through a food processor. Wait until after the wort boil is over and the wort has cooled to 200°F (93°C) to add your fruit.

Cover the kettle with its lid and keep the wort and fruit between 160°F and 180°F (71°-82°C) for twenty minutes to pasteurize it. Stir the wort occasionally. Don't boil your fruit unless you want fruit haze. Keep the fruit pulp in the fermenter during the primary fermentation.

When making a fruit beer from real fruit, add it to your secondary fermenter. If you add it to your primary fermenter, the escaping CO_2 will carry off some of the aroma and flavor.

You can use blended, crushed, whole or frozen fruit. Be sure to USE A BLOW-OFF TUBE instead of an airlock/bubbler because fermenting fruit WILL clog your airlock and blow it off halfway across the room.

For a nice fruit pectin haze special effect, boil your fruit (raspberries for instance) for 5-15 minutes. Then pour the fruit into your secondary fermenter before transferring your beer to it.

Fruit flavors will be stronger if you add the fruit to the secondary fermentation. But you still have to pasteurize it to prevent bacterial contamination. Mash or food process your fruit and add water if the pulp is not juicy enough to stir easily.

Slowly raise the temperature of the fruit pulp to 180°F to pasteurize it, stirring frequently. Cover your pot and let the pulp rest for 20 minutes. Let it cool to room temperature before adding it to your secondary fermenter. Add one or two weeks to the secondary fermentation period.

You can skip pasteurization of your fruit if you are adding it to beer that is high in alcohol - over five percent by volume. Be super thorough when you clean the fruit and sanitize all the equipment you use to pulp it.

Add fruit flavor extracts at the very end of the brewing process. When you're ready to bottle, before you rack your beer, add a small, carefully measured amount of extract to a one-cup sample of your beer. Swirl them together and taste.

Keep adding the same amount of extract until you reach the flavor you are aiming for. Keep careful notes of how much total extract you added and multiply that total by the number of cups of beer that you've brewed. There are 80 cups or half pints in a 5-gallon (19L) batch. Put the extract in your bottling bucket and rack your beer on top of it.

Chapter 5: Common yeast strains and characteristics

YEAST/ MICROBE TYPE/ ORIGIN		PREDOMINANT FLAVOR CHARACTER	BEER USAGE/ STYLE GUIDELINE
American Yeasts	Ale	Clean fermenting flavors. These yeasts ferment strongly and quickly. They let hop flavors and aromas take center stage.	Most all-American styles. Pale Ales, IPAs, Amber Ales. Also great for big Stouts.
English Yeasts	Ale	Slower to ferment. Favors slightly fruity/ester production. These yeasts are great at promoting malty flavored beers.	English IPAs, Bitters, Pale Ales, Brown Ales, and Stouts. Excellent for Porters and ESBs.
Belgian Yeasts	Ale	Known for their phenol production, complex ester profiles. A very unique range of flavors, often with a high alcohol tolerance. Strong fermenting.	Trappist and Abbey Ales. Belgian Pale all the way to strong Belgian Triple. Excellent choices for Belgian dark strong ales.
German and Yeasts	Ale Lager	Wide range of temperature fermentation temperatures. Typically very clean fermentation. Known for super crisp and bright beer flavors.	Kölsch, Altbier, and Bocks. Lager yeasts are excellent choices for Pilsner styles.

SPECIAL APPLICATION YEASTS/MICROBES

Hefeweizen Ale Yeast	A German style well known for its clove and banana flavors; use in wheat-forward worts.	Hefeweizen, Dunkel, Weizen.
Saison Yeast	Unique French/Belgian yeast rumored to be derived from historical white wine yeast. Ferments beer to very dry levels. Interesting flavors of fruit, peppercorns, and more.	Saison.
Brettanomyces	A wide range of ale yeasts that are a different evolutionary arm than traditional brewer's yeast. Some produce acidic, funky flavors reminiscent of leather and tobacco. Other strains are known for tropical fruit flavors.	Belgian ales, most commonly the Lambic styles. However, also used as a flavor enhancer in cleaner ales. Often used in combination with other yeasts but can be used alone for unique beers.
Lactobacillus	Bacteria that produces lactic acid. A clean-tasting sour/tart acid.	Berliner Weisse.
Pediococcus	Bacteria that produces lactic acid along with other "funky" flavors. Not recommended as a stand-alone microbe. Must be co-pitched with Brettanomyces.	Often part of a blend for making complex sour ales.

Types of yeast

Two of the biggest categories of brewer's yeast are ale and lager. Ale yeasts tend to want to ferment warmer, typically in the 65° to 72°F/18° to 22°C range. Lager yeasts, on the other hand, ferment well at 50° to 55°F/10° to 13°C. As you now know, the lower the fermentation temperature, the less expressive the yeast strain is. This behavior is why lager beers are so well recognized for their clean, neutral tastes. The cooler fermentation suppresses much of the yeast character. There are limits to this temperature/character relationship, however. Trying to ferment at 50°F/10°C with an ale yeast strain, which has an optimal temperature of 70°F/21°C, usually won't work. The ale yeast, sensing the colder temperature, will fall asleep and go dormant, leaving your wort unfermented.

when you purchase your beer kit, you often will face a choice on yeast. The manufacturer of the kit will provide recommended strains, from which we think you should choose for your first batch. If you want to try a different yeast strain than the ones suggested in the recipe, we recommend using the rule of thumb about the origin of the style you are trying to ferment. That is, if you want to make a great German Altbier, select a German ale yeast. If a hoppy American Pale Ale is what you are planning to brew, choose the American ale yeast. That's not to say you can't mix and match. As you brew more, try different yeasts with the same base recipe kit. There are so many yeast choices, you will likely never run out of options when brewing one kit or recipe over and over again.

Primary Fermentation

After you pitch your selected yeast strain into the wort, the yeast will start to go to work. Within 12 to 48 hours, you should start to see bubbles coming through your airlock. If you see no activity after 48 hours, you will want to check that the lid has sealed properly. When you look into the beer, if there is no foam at the top or yeast movement in the beer, you will want to pitch a new packet of yeast.

For best fermentation results with ale strains, store your fermentor in a place where the temperature does not fluctuate greatly during the day and night and stays within the yeast strain's recommended temperature range; it's also important to store the fermentor out of direct light, natural or artificial. Light destroys hop aroma compounds, turning them into skunky aromas. If you have ever had "skunked beer," you know exactly what those flavors taste like. This reaction is also called "light-struck beer." An interior closet or an unused bathtub is a good place to store your beer. Do not use your garage or back porch as a place to store your fermentor. These are places where the temperature will change drastically over the course of a day and are not safe places for your beer. Once you find a dark place that stays pretty much the same temperature all day long, make sure it can stay there for at least two weeks. In cooler rooms, you can wrap your beer in a blanket to help insulate it against temperature swings.

Your wort contains sugars that, at first, feed the yeast as it grows and multiplies in number. Eventually, the yeast slows its multiplication and metabolizes the sugars into alcohol and carbon dioxide. All this activity is called the primary fermentation. The most active part of this ferment will last 3 to 5 days, depending on the temperature, strength of the beer, and amount of yeast added. During this phase, a large band of foam, called krausen, will form on top of the wort; it's perfectly normal. (If you are using a glass fermentor on your first batch, you will be able to see the fermentation even before there are bubbles in the airlock.) The carbon dioxide leaving your fermentor will produce bubbles in the airlock at a rapid rate. After some time, you will see all the bubbles in the airlock slow drastically or stop altogether, which is a good sign that fermentation is ending. You now no longer have wort—you've made beer!

When fermentation ends, it is a good practice to let the beer sit in the fermentor for another 4 or 5 days. It's common practice to allow the beer to sit after the most active signs of fermentation have passed. The conventional wisdom is that, while the yeast is done fermenting, there are still subtle flavor components that develop from the yeast that don't normally result in visual cues. This extra waiting period ensures you're letting your yeast put the finishing touches on your ferment. Expect your fermentation practice to last two weeks generally. There is no need to transfer a finished beer to a different container (secondary fermentor) just to let it sit or clarify. It will do those things just fine in the primary fermentor. It is also okay to let the beer get a little cooler during this phase.

The surest way to tell if your beer is done fermenting and ready to bottle is to use a hydrometer. A hydrometer is a tool that measures the density of sugar in a solution. A beer hydrometer used at the end of the ferment should provide similar readings at least 2 or 3 days in a row. If your readings are staying put, you'll know your beer is done. Homebrew beer ingredient kits or recipes will state what the target final gravity should be. This target will help you decide if the beer is done and ready for the next steps. Don't be afraid to use it. As long as you sanitize all equipment that touches the beer when you are getting a sample to test in the hydrometer, you will not infect your beer. When you're done testing the gravity, don't put the sample back in the fermentor. You can pour it down your sink—or drink it!

Using your hydrometer, you can calculate the alcohol by volume percentage (ABV) in your beer. Before fermentation, you need to take a reading of the Original Gravity (OG) of your wort. Once you have a reading, mark it down. After fermentation is over, you can take your Final Gravity (FG) reading. Plugging these two numbers into the formula below will give you your estimated ABV.

The formula is (OG − FG) × 131 = ABV.

For example, if your OG was 1.045 and your FG was 1.010, the ABV of your beer would be 4.59%.

(1.045 − 1.010) × 131 = 4.59%.

Secondary Fermentation

A secondary fermentation is employed when you plan to add something to the finished beer after the primary fermentation is done. True secondary ferment occurs only when you are adding something that contains more sugar, like fruit or syrup. You can use a secondary fermentor even when there will be no sugar added, like in the case of adding some oak chips/cubes or bourbon or any other non-sugar-based additive. Keep in mind oak and small amounts of flavorings can go into your primary fermentor, too, as long as you have the volume to hold it. If you don't have the space, use a secondary fermentor. You wouldn't want to add 2 gallons/7.5 liters of mixed berries to a 5-gallon/19-liter batch of beer in a 6-gallon/23-liter bucket.

The length of time you use a secondary fermentor to add flavors should be gauged based on flavor. If you are adding oak, for example, it takes time for the oak flavors to get picked up in the beer. Try small samples occasionally to determine if it's time to move on to bottling the beer. If you are adding fruit or other sugars, you will need to check the final gravity again to be sure the beer is done with the secondary fermentation. Expect a slightly higher gravity now than you had at the end of primary fermentation. Overall, use a secondary fermentor judiciously. You can quite frequently skip a secondary fermentor in favor of reducing oxygen exposure and lessening the risk of additional microbe contamination.

Bottling and Conditioning

This phase is the last one in the homebrewing beer process before, you know, drinking it. Getting this part right means you'll soon be drinking quite possibly the freshest beer you've ever had. The most important part of this process is to sanitize every item that will touch the finished beer. We want to take the utmost care of the beer as it is transferred into the bottles.

Clean and sanitize all your bottles and bottle caps. A 5-gallon/19-liter batch normally requires two cases of 12-fluid ounce/355-milliliter bottles. That's 48 bottles. If that number seems pretty daunting, many brewers move to the 22-fluid ounce/650-milliliter "bomber" bottle, as you'll only need 24 of those. Brand-new bottles might only need a rinse in hot water followed by a quick soak in sanitizer. If you are reusing bottles, however, be sure they are totally clean before sanitizing them. First, look in the bottle to be sure there is no beer residue or mold from the last beer that was in it. A good practice when reusing bottles is to be sure they are fully rinsed after you drink the beer that was in them before. This limits the amount of effort that has to be devoted to cleaning used bottles. If there is some residue in the bottles, use a bottle brush to get it all out. Don't fear reusing bottles, though, as it is a great way to cut expenses and save money for your next batch of ingredients.

Finally, sanitize your racking/transfer cane and tubing. And don't forget to sanitize the bottling bucket, spigot, and filling wand.

Initiating Carbonation

After fermentation is complete, your wort has been turned into beer. When you open the fermentor, it most certainly will smell like beer. If you taste a sample for a specific gravity reading, you'll notice that, while it tastes like beer, it is probably pretty flat and uncarbonated.

To get the carbonation, you need to add a little sugar back into the beer. This sugar will give the yeast in the beer something new to eat. Remember all the bubbling the airlock did on your fermentor during the fermentation phase? Well, this time, instead of letting that carbon dioxide gas escape through the airlock, you will trap it in the bottle by capping the bottle. As the yeast ferments the small amount of sugar, the carbon dioxide will pressurize the bottle slightly, and it will eventually dissolve into the beer. This process is called natural carbonation.

The sugar you are about to introduce to the beer is called priming sugar. Any sugar can be priming sugar, so the term "sugar" is used generally here. Normally, for a 5-gallon/19-liter batch of beer, you will need 4 to 4.5 ounces (by weight)/113 to 128 grams of table sugar. Some homebrew kits come with what is called corn sugar. Both types of sugar are fine and don't have an impact on beer flavor. Corn sugar requires just a little bit more than table sugar (4.5 to 5 ounces/128 to 142 grams).

The priming sugar needs to be prepared in a certain way before being added to your beer. You don't want to just add the dried form of the sugar into the beer for two reasons. First, you want to sanitize the sugar by boiling it. (Remember to sanitize everything that touches the beer.) Second, you can't guarantee that the powdered sugar will dissolve in the beer on its own fast enough. By boiling it in some water, you make a solution that is more predictable to mix into the beer.

Why is this important? Preparing a primary sugar solution ensures that every bottle of beer gets the same amount of sugar, which ensures that every bottle has the same carbonation level. Inconsistent sugar amounts in the bottles mean some bottles might be flat, some just right, and some over-carbonated. There is no magic formula for how much water to sugar there is. You are just making a simple solution. Too much water dilutes the beer, so just 16 fluid ounces/473 milliliters of water is fine. Put that water in a small saucepan and stir in the sugar you measured out by weight. Bring it to a boil with occasional stirring. It doesn't have to boil hard or very long; 15 minutes is all it takes. Once you have that sugar solution made, you're ready to start bottling. Once the priming sugar is dissolved and you've boiled it to sanitize, you can transfer it directly into the bottling bucket. You should do this prior to racking the beer into the bucket. That way, as the beer transfers from fermentor into the bottling bucket, it will mix on its own. No further agitation on your part should be required.

A few suppliers make small drops of sugar called carbonation drops. They look like small white candies, because that is what they are. They are designed to be added to your empty bottles and dissolve in the beer fairly rapidly. The idea behind carbonation drops is that each tablet will carbonate one bottle of beer. You simply add one to each bottle before filling the bottle with the beer from the bottling bucket. These carbonation drops/tabs work okay most of the time. We have heard of a few stories where the tablets don't fully dissolve or leave a weird residue and the beer doesn't fully carbonate in those bottles. Although it is fun to experiment with these types of innovations, we recommend you prepare the priming sugar solution and add it to your first batch or two as we detailed because it has had more consistent results than the tablets.

Filling the Bottles

After your priming sugar solution is ready and your bottles and bottling bucket and equipment are sanitized, it is time to get that beer into the bucket. First, dump your solution of priming sugar into the bucket. It is okay if the solution is still hot from the boil. It's a small volume compared to the whole batch of beer, so the temperature will equalize pretty quickly in this next phase. Place your fermentor on a countertop or table. Position your bottling bucket on the floor below it, as you'll use gravity to transfer the beer from the fermentor to the bottling bucket.

Get your racking/siphon equipment ready. Attach the tubing to the racking cane, and fill it with clean water from the tap. Use a low flow of water and take your time. It can be tricky to fill the tube—it may take some practice. Once you have filled the tubing with water, put the straight end of the racking cane into the beer/fermentor. Then, slowly drop the tubing end down into the bottling bucket. The water will flow out of the cane into the bucket and start a siphon, pulling the beer into the bucket as well. Immediately after the flow of beer starts, lift the racking cane off the bottom of the fermentor so you don't pull too much yeast. You should see fairly clear beer running through the tube after lifting the cane.

Watch as the beer mixes in with the priming sugar solution. Have no fear—as long as the beer swirls gently into the bucket, the sugar mixes in well. Avoid the temptation to sanitize a long spoon and stir the beer. You want to limit oxygen uptake as much as you can. Excessive oxygen pickup will stale the beer. You should also be sure that the distance of the fermentor to the bottling bucket is such that the beer runs out of the racking tubing into the bottom of the bottling bucket. You don't want to splash the beer into the bucket due to the aforementioned beer staling.

Once all the beer has been transferred, you are ready to start filling bottles. You'll want to use a table or countertop to rest your filled bottling bucket. Most bottling bucket setups will have a spigot and a bottle-filling wand. A small piece of tubing usually connects these two items together, although some wands can get connected to the spigot. The purpose of the wand is to deliver the beer to the bottom of the bottle with minimal splashing (there's that pesky oxygen/staling issue again) and to create the perfect headspace. You need to have a small headspace in each bottle. The right-size headspace aids in getting the right amount of carbonation. Too big or too small a headspace and the beer won't carbonate at all.

To fill a bottle, you simply take a bottle (cleaned and sanitized, right?) and slide the opening up from the base of the filling wand. The base of the wand has a spring-loaded valve in it. When you push the inside base of the bottle up against the wand, the beer starts to flow into the bottle. Just as the beer reaches the top opening of the bottle, you will pull the bottle away. The spring-loaded valve will re-engage and the beer will stop flowing. When you pull the bottle off the wand completely, you'll see that the perfect amount of headspace is created. Once a bottle is filled, you can cap it.

Chapter 6: How to create distilled wine

The last section for us on this journey is a detailed chapter on how to distil wine at home.

Wine is one of the most loved alcoholic beverage in the world, a lot of people love wine for varying reasons, and it is only natural for anyone who loves wine to learn how to distil at home.

This section will be a fun last chapter, so get your aprons ready, and let's dive in!

First, you will need the following materials:

Dutch oven

Dish soap

Water

Towel

Sponge

Copper still

Wine

Glass jars (clean ones)

Glass containers

Step One

Get a copper alembic pot that is mostly used by beginners and professionals alike. The pots are available in a variety of sizes, but I will advise that you use the 1-liter pot, which is equivalent to 0.26 US Gal. you can also use the 2-liter size, which is 0.53 US Gal as they are also manageable when used for distilling purposes at home.

These alembic pots can be purchased online, and if you haven't done this before, you might also want to consider a teakettle. A teakettle will serve as an experimental tool to distil small batches of wine first before making more significant purchases.

Step Two

Put the still in a pot, and this pot has to be large enough to contain both still and water. The Dutch ovens are high for this because they can hold up to two litres of still.

Step Three

Now fill the pot up to a three-quarter level with the water, you can pour tap water into the Dutch oven but don't make it excessively full. If it is too full, it will overflow and ruin the entire process.

Step Four

Next, pour the wine into the still (not the Dutch oven). It should be three-quarters full of wine and try not to fill it beyond this because you must be mindful of bubbles that will show up at the top when the still is heated. Please note that for your choice of wine, you can use store-bought wine, and the amount you will require is based on the still you will use.

After getting better at distilling, you can try this process out with homemade wine instead of store-bought.

Step Five

The next step entails running a tube from the pot o the condenser by first placing the lid on the still. The condenser comes out of the lid's top, and it has a spout that can be attached to the copper tube. Place the end of the tube in the spout in a separate bucket (don't worry as all of these parts are included with the still when you make a still purchase, you will see these other parts).

While some condensers have different spouts, the one facing downwards is attached to a tap. Attach the second tube to the upward spout and set the other end in your sink. If you discover that you don't have these parts, you can create your condenser coil using a copper tube and bucket.

Step Six

Next, you will add cold water to the condenser. Fill the bucket (not the still) with cold water so it can chill the evaporated wine into a liquid. At this point, the condenser tube should be inside the bucket with the spout on the side. So long the tube is stuck on the spout, the bucket will not leak water.

If the whole set up doesn't fit well on the still, combine ½ cups of rye flour with three tablespoons of water and place the mixture on the loose area. As the still receives heat, it will create a seal.

Step Seven

Place a glass under the spout, also have lots of glasses close by because you will have to rotate them to get the distillation as it drips. The first glass can be a larger jar or bottle as the first millilitres you get wouldn't taste right, so that you will discard it.

Step Eight

Now you are ready to heat up the wine. The first thing to do is to turn the heat high until the alcohol drips. Make sure you keep a close eye on the still because if the water gets too hot, it will boil, and this will make the distillation drip into the glass even faster.

If the drip is too fast, it means you will get less alcohol in each drip. You can always adjust the drip speed to your preferred level as you practice distilling.

Also, do not use an open flame as an electric burner indoors is a safe option. You can also use a propane or natural gas burner (outdoors).

Step Nine

Now you have to lower the heat so distillation can continue, so the water temperature should be at 78 degrees (you can place a thermostat inside the condenser's spout). Always watch the drip speed to keep track of the temperature, and when the distillate drips (one or three times every second), it is a sign that you're still is at the right temperature.

Step Ten

Check your distillate and change the bottles, but for you to do this, you must frequently check to see how the wine is doing. To avoid spills, replace the bottles, and this will improve the quality of the wine as it drips. Also, have a taste at this point to ensure you are on track with the process.

Step Eleven

The foul-smelling distillate should be thrown out, and this is often the first 50 millilitre (it is undrinkable). This early 50 millilitre has lots of acetone and wood alcohol; it is poisonous and has a rancid smell. This liquid is also known as the foreshot, and it isn't right.

Step Twelve

After the foreshot drains out, you will get the drinkable alcohol next. You can tell it is drinkable because of its fruity smell (it will smell like the fruits/herbs used in the wine).

Now the still is even hotter and may drip at a faster level, so collect the small liquid glasses and switch them as they fill up. You will most likely get 2 litres of quality wine (could be less but around this number).

Step Thirteen

The distillate will start to look milky, throw it out when it loses its colour. Also, smell it and detect the aroma, when the odour is out, the wine is mixed with water and undrinkable alcohol, throw it out.

Cleaning

Now that your wine is ready, you have to clean up afterward.

Remember that what you are distilling will be consumed as such the process for creation and post-distilling matters in ensuring proper hygiene.

Start by turning off the heat by providing the burner is turned off. Then give the still some time to get cold and move the wine to a cool cellar or cabinet.

Remove the still and be careful with dropping it so it doesn't break, and you can use it another time.

Remove the still's condenser and lid, pull the cover off and wash the still with soap and water. You can also clean the copper pots with salt and vinegar because it mostly starts to look green after use.

Now you can chill at your favourite corner in your home with your perfectly distilled wine.

With this practical chapter on wine distillation, we have come to the end of an exciting and enlightening journey.

Chapter 7: Mixing up for a beer

Beer is a trendy alcoholic beverage, as regardless of where you are in the world, you will surely find a unique type of beer consumed by the locals.

With a few ingredients and some materials, you can brew beer at home in mini-batches.

If you enjoy the process of creating beer, you can do it repeatedly until it becomes a full-time hobby.

Here is a list of ingredients and materials you will need for beer processing:

Kitchen thermometer

Bottling container (get an empty container, clean water bottle or a food-grade plastic bucket)

A filter (the type that strains grains)

A brew pot

Bottles for your beer

Clear poly-vinyl tubing (3 feet of 3/8" (this will aid siphoning and fermentation)

Rolling pin (aids with crushing the grain)

Large funnel

A container of bottled water (3 gallons) will provide water for the beer, and also it can be a container used for the fermentation process.

3/8 cup of sugar (suitable for bottling)

3 lbs light dried malt extract

1 oz brewer pellet hops (Northern)

One pkg brewer's yeast

8 oz crystal malt (crushed)

With these ingredients and materials, you are ready to get started! Please note that there could be variants of beer that can be made at home.

This recipe is just one of many and will introduce you to the idea, as you do I regularly you can devise new processes and mixtures.

Step One

The first step is to crush the grains. Place the 8 ounces of crystal malt in a large freezer bag. With a rolling pin, crush the grains and try not to make it very smooth. You are not supposed to get a flour-like texture, just a coarse texture, as the aim is to break the grains. When you decide to take this beer-making process seriously, you can purchase malt mill from stores that are designed specifically for this process.

Step Two

Steeping is referred to as the brewing term for the extraction of all the goodness in the grains. Pour ½ gallons of water from your 3-gallon water bottle and mark the 2 ½ water level.

Then pour 2 ½ of the remaining water into your brew pot (make sure you leave at least 3 inches to the top). Then add the grains you crushed and turn on the heat to medium-high while bringing the temperature to 150 or 155 degrees.

Turn off the heat, cover the brew pot, and let the process commence inside the pot (leave it like this for 30 minutes). With a strainer, remove the spent grain (don't worry if you still have some in the pot).

Step Three

The content of the brew pot should boil, and afterward, it should be removed from the heat as you stir in the malt extract. Put it back on the heat to boil, but at this stage, you must pay close attention to the pot so you can avoid overcooking the content. If you have a boil-over, you will have to clean up the sticky mess, and it isn't a pleasant experience.

After controlling the boil, add 2/3 oz of the hop pellets to the boiling pot and leave it to boil for 60 minutes (this will help you get the best out of the bittering nature of the hops). Place your filter in the boiling pot so it is sanitized for about 15 minutes (you will use it later).

Turn off the heat after 60 minutes and add the rest of the hop pellets. Cover the pot, let the new hops steep for 10 minutes as they will add to the flavor and aroma of your beer.

Step Four

Now you can work on the airlock. You can use a commercial airlock or create one from clear vinyl tubing with one end to the cap and the other in a cup of water. Commercial airlocks can be bought at stores for $1 (including a starter kit).

But if you don't want to use commercial airlocks, you can drill a hole of about 3/8" in the water bottle cap. The airlock will fit the hole, and the whole idea of this process is to allow the carbon dioxide produced during fermentation escape without air from outside, getting inside.

Step Five

Now at this stage, you have wort. Wort is "Unfermented beer," and it has to be cooled. An excellent method for cooling is to have a cold bath in the sink to submerse the brew pot (not entirely). Add some ice to the bath as it will help to accelerate the cooling process, then swirl the pot in the cold liquid.

When all sides of the pot appear cool (when you can touch it), you know it is ready for the next stage. But first, at this point, sanitation is essential because the beer is almost available for consumption.

Whatever comes in contact with the wort must be sanitized, or else you will make the mixture develop critters that multiply in the wort giving your beer an undesirable flavor. Sanitize everything you use with the wort, such as your funnel, by soaking them in a solution of 1 tablespoon of bleach for 30 minutes.

Step Six

Start pouring the cooled wort through the sanitized strainer and funnel into the fermentation bottle. The total volume of the fermenter should be 2 ½ gallons, but your brew pot was huge and made it easier for you to boil ½ gallon you will have to compensate for the evaporation that happened while it was cooking.

If you need to add more water from the gallon, then you can use tap water or water from the ½ gallon you poured off previously.

Step Seven

Now you are ready to pitch the yeast. Pitching the yeast is a brewing term for the addition of yeast to the unfermented wort. If the wort (the one in your fermenter) is at room temperature, then you can pitch your yeast. You will know if it is at room temperature when the sides are warm enough to touch. If the sides are not warm enough, then you should allow it to cool down before pitching the yeast.

Please note that most of the time, a package of brewer's yeast contains enough yeast for a 5-gallon batch. Don't pour the entire content into the fermenter, use about half of the pack, you can add a little bit more, but it shouldn't be lesser than the required amount.

Step Eight

Now you will have to leave the yeast to work over 7 to 10 days as it converts sugars in the wort to alcohol and carbon dioxide. Put the fermenter in a cool and dark place, it doesn't have to be a very dark place, but this is also a crucial part of the process. Do not place it under direct sunlight.

The process of fermentation is always enjoyable to observe; however, you shouldn't worry if nothing happens within 12 to 24 hours as, after this time, you will see foaming and bubbles that escape from the airlock. After the 7 to 10 day period, the fermented sugars will complete its conversion through the yeast.

Step Nine

Now you have your beer!

But we are not completely done at this point. If you drink the beer, now the taste will be flat; as such, you must complete the process through priming. Priming entails adding a measured amount of additional fermented sugars before bottling commences. The active yeast in your beer will convert the added sugars to carbon dioxide in the bottle.

The carbon dioxide will not escape the bottle, thus leading o the creation of carbonated water. Then boil 3/8 of sugar (which is ¼ cup and two tablespoons) you might want to use corn sugar or table sugar all in one cup of water for 5 minutes. Cover the mixture, allow it cool down and pour into a sanitized container that can hold your beer (this can be another large water bottle or empty plastic bucket).

Take the beer from the fermenter into the bottling container (please be careful while doing this) Now your beer is primed! What should you do next?

Bottling!

Step Ten

When you start brewing beer at home, remember to get beer bottles for the final stage of the process. You will also need caps or a keg that will contain your finished product. There are several options for the first time you brew, so feel free to experiment as soon enough you will stick to a particular bottling choice.

You can also purchase empty bottles and caps, or get reusable bottles and caps. Champagne bottles are great alternatives as well; what matters the most is that the bottles are sanitized before usage. You can soak the bottles in diluted bleach for 30 minutes and rinse with clean water.

Step Eleven

The next step is known as aging, and it entails keeping the beers in bottles for at least seven days, so the fermentation takes place inside the bottle. This process will also carbonate the beer, just ensure that the beer is placed in a cool dark place for a minimum of 7 days and a maximum of 10 days. Do not open the bottle too early, and don't put it in the fridge yet.

During this time, the beer will start to become more transparent because the suspended yeast will settle at the bottom of the bottle.

Step Twelve

Drink your beer!

After the ten days, you can place the beer in the fridge, so it's chilled. Open the bottle and pour yourself a glass. The beer will taste excellently well, and you will have developed a tasty brew.

When beer tastes that good, the fun can begin with friends and family at home, which is one of the critical objectives of this book: to empower you with information that will help you do things the right way the first time.

Recipes

Hibiscus-Blackberry Wine

Ingredients:

- Fresh water – 12 cups
- Sugar – 1 kilogram
- Blackberries – 1½ kilograms
- Hibiscus flowers – 4oz
- Sage – 2oz
- Campden tablets – 2
- Wine Yeast – 1 teaspoon
- Yeast nutrient – 1 teaspoon

Directions

1. Boil your water
2. Add in the sugar and the hibiscus then remove from the heat source.
3. Use a sieve to strain your mixture.
4. Extract the blackberry juice and add it into the hibiscus mixture.
5. Next, crush one campden tablet and add it into the mixture.

6. Add the yeast into the herbal mixture.

7. Let the herbal mixture rest for around 3hr.

8. Next, add in the yeast nutrient and ensure to mix it properly.

9. Leave the mixture to rest for 7 days but stir it from time to time.

10. From then on, let the mixture rest until a month is over.

11. Add in your other campden tablet.

12. Your hibiscus-blackberry flavored wine is now ready to drink at your pace. Follow this preparation method for other wine recipes unless stated otherwise.

Hyssop-Lemon Balm Wine

Ingredients:

- Fresh water – 5 liters
- Brown granulated sugar – 2 kilograms
- Wine yeast – 1 teaspoon
- Hyssop – 2 cups
- Sage – ½ cup
- Lemon balm – 1 cup

Directions

1. For this particular recipe, you need to leave it for a longer period – around 5mths to 9mths before you can term it ready to drink. Although you can take a sip before this period, it will not have acquired the wine flavor you desire, with a high probability of it tasting like hooch.

Oak-Grape Wine

Ingredients:

- Fresh water – 5 liters
- Grape leaves – 2 kilograms
- Oak chips – 2 cups
- White sugar – 8 cups
- Wine yeast – 1 teaspoon

Directions

1. You can expect a tangy taste that is, at the same time, fruity, not just because of the grape leaves but also because oak gives the wine a vanilla-like flavor.

-

Dandelion-Orange Wine

Ingredients:

- Fresh water – 5 liters
- Dandelion flowers (without stalks) – 20 cups
- Fresh oranges – 3 large
- Fresh lemon – 1 large
- Sugar – 2 kilograms
- Wine yeast – 1 teaspoon

Directions

1. Make a point of picking your dandelion flowers, or any other flowers you use for your wine, in a location free from pesticides.

-

Horseradish Molasses Wine

Ingredients:

- Fresh water – 5 liters
- Vinegar – ½ liter
- Molasses – 1 liter
- Horseradish root (chopped) – 1 cup
- Ginger (grated) – 1 tablespoon

Directions

1. This wine will make your blocked nasal passage open, as you enjoy its uplifting effect.

Tomato Wine

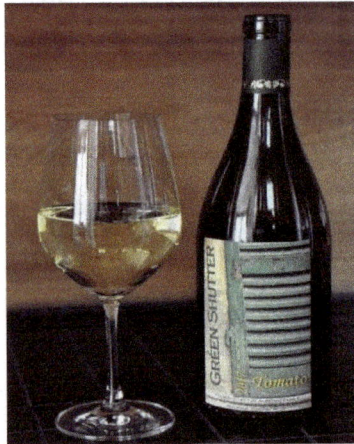

Ingredients

- 7kg x tomatoes
- 1kg raisins
- 15 liters x water
- 4kg x sugar
- 1 x Red wine yeast

Directions

1. Sanitise all equipment.
2. Wash the tomatoes.
3. Cut them into small pieces.
4. Wrap the tomatoes in a straining bag and squeeze all the juice out into a bucket.
5. Fill the bucket with 15 liters of hot water.
6. Place the straining bag into the water to extract as much flavor as possible.
7. Put the raisins and sugar in and stir until the sugar has dissolved.
8. Cover with a cloth and tie closed and leave in a cool ark place for 24 hours.
9. Remove the cloth and stir everything.
10. Add the yeast and place the cloth back on the bucket.
11. Stir twice a day.
12. Allow a week for this process.
13. Filter off the solids and place the liquid either in anew container or clean out the one in use.
14. Replace the cloth with a sealable lid.
15. Ensure the airlock and lid seal the unit.
16. Allow to ferment until the airlock stops bubbling.
17. Crush two Campden tablets and place in the liquid.

18. Allow the yeast to settle then siphon off the clear wine.
19. You may have to siphon again if it is still cloudy.
20. Once the wine is clear then you can bottle it.

Strawberry Wine

Ingredients

- 1kg x fresh strawberries
- 1kg x sugar
- 5liters x pure water
- 1 x Wine yeast

Directions

1. Boil the water and add the sugar. Allow to cool.
2. Mash the strawberries and add to the sugar water.
3. Stir vigorously and add the yeast.
4. Cover with a cloth and tie it with string or elastic.
5. Place in a cool area.
6. Stir twice a day for a week.
7. Remove the pulp using a sieve.
8. Filter the remaining pieces using a coffee filter or straining bag.
9. Put the juice in a carboy or clean sanitised bucket and seal with an airlock on the lid.
10. Wait until the airlock becomes silent and carefully siphon off the wine.
11. Leave to settle and siphon again.

12. You will have to judge if you need to siphon any more, but you should be able to bottle your product that will have a nice rose color.

Orange Wine

Ingredients

- 10-12 Navel or Seville oranges.
- 5 liters pure water.
- 2.5 kg sugar.

1 x Wine yeast

Directions

1. Grate or cut off the zest (colored part of the peel), of the oranges.
2. Juice the oranges but do not add any of the white as it is bitter.
3. Cut out any of the fruit and add that to the juice.
4. Boil the water and add the sugar.
5. Stir vigorously until the sugar has dissolved and allow to cool. Cover with a cloth.
6. Add the juice, zest and pulp and stir.
7. Add the yeast. Cover up with a cloth and tie it on.

8. Leave in a cool area for a week but stir twice daily to get the flavors mixed in.
9. Use a sieve to remove the large pulp then filter out the pieces.
10. Place in a carboy or bucket with an airlock fitted.
11. Leave to ferment.
12. Once the airlock is silent then siphon of the wine from the lees.
13. Add a campden tablet either now or before first siphoning.

14. Bottle and store in a cool dark area.

CPSIA information can be obtained
at www.ICGtesting.com
Printed in the USA
BVHW011207190321
602997BV00004B/227